Pictures of the World

Pictures of the World

Three Views of Life, the Universe, and Everything

Scott Steinkerchner

AND

Peter Hunter

FOREWORD BY
Peter C. Phan

CASCADE *Books* • Eugene, Oregon

PICTURES OF THE WORLD
Three Views of Life, the Universe, and Everything

Copyright © 2018 Scott Steinkerchner and Peter Hunter. All rights reserved. Except for brief quotations in critical publications or reviews, no part of this book may be reproduced in any manner without prior written permission from the publisher. Write: Permissions, Wipf and Stock Publishers, 199 W. 8th Ave., Suite 3, Eugene, OR 97401.

Cascade Books
An Imprint of Wipf and Stock Publishers
199 W. 8th Ave., Suite 3
Eugene, OR 97401

www.wipfandstock.com

PAPERBACK ISBN: 978-1-5326-1805-5
HARDCOVER ISBN: 978-1-4982-4327-8
EBOOK ISBN: 978-1-4982-4326-1

Cataloguing-in-Publication data:

Names: Steinkerchner, Scott. | Hunter, Peter. | Phan, Peter C. (foreword)

Title: Pictures of the world : three views of life, the universe, and everything / by Scott Steinkerchner and Peter Hunter.

Description: Eugene, OR: Cascade Books, 2018 | Includes bibliographical references.

Identifiers: ISBN 978-1-5326-1805-5 (paperback) | ISBN 978-1-4982-4327-8 (hardcover) | ISBN 978-1-4982-4326-1 (ebook)

Subjects: LCSH: Life. | Thomas, Aquinas, Saint, 1225?–1274. | Tsong-kha-pa Blo-bzang-grags-pa, 1357–1419. | Pinker, Steven, 1954–. | Christianity. | Buddhism | Naturalism

Classification: LCC BL80.3 P44 2018 (print) | LCC BL80.3 (ebook)

Scripture quotations are from New Revised Standard Version Bible, copyright © 1989 National Council of the Churches of Christ in the United States of America. Used by permission. All rights reserved worldwide.

Photo credits—Figure 1.1: Uoaei1 via Wikimedia Commons, licensed through Creative Commons CC BY-SA 4.0; Figure 1.2: Lawrence Lew OP, © English Province of the Order of Preachers, used by permission; Figure 1.3, Stephen Murray © Mapping Gothic France, The Trustees of Columbia University, Media Center for Art History, Department of Art History and Archaeology, used by permission; Figure 2.1,2.4: Scott Steinkerchner OP, © Dominicans, Province of St. Albert the Great, used by permission; Figures 2.2,2.3: Dave Moore, © Aquinas Institute of Theology, used by permission; Figure 3.1: M. Garde—Self work (Original by: José-Manuel Benitos), licensed through Creative Commons, CC BY-SA 3.0; Figure 3.2: Painting by Salvador Dali, photo courtesy of WikiArt.com, Fair Use license

Manufactured in the U.S.A.   07/23/18

Contents

Foreword by Peter C. Phan | vii

Introduction | xi

1. Thomas Aquinas: A Christian Picture of the World | 1
2. Tsongkhapa: A Buddhist Picture of the World | 22
3. Steven Pinker: A Naturalist Picture of the World | 45
4. In Comparison | 63
   The Human Person | 63
   What Is Real? How Do We Know? | 66
   Consciousness and Free Will | 74
   Arguments For and Against Creation | 83
   The Basis of Morality | 94
   Gender Equality | 97
   Homosexuality and Gay Marriage | 102
   Research Using Human Embryonic Stem Cells | 108
5. Learning from Others | 114
   Original Sin and Our Need for Salvation | 116
   The Extent of the Salvation Won by Jesus Christ | 127
   A Vision of Heaven | 146
   What Have We Learned? | 154

Epilogue | 156
Works Cited | 161

Foreword
Peter C. Phan

What do the thirteenth-century Christian Thomas Aquinas, the fourteenth-century Tibetan Buddhist Tsong-kha-pa Blo-bzang-grags-pa, and the twentieth-century naturalist experimental psychologist Steven Pinker have in common that would warrant a meaningful comparison among them? How indeed can a theistic theologian, a non-theistic monk, and an atheistic scientist living across centuries and continents, in markedly different cultures, and holding diametrically divergent religious views, be possibly brought together to contribute to the common fund of wisdom that may guide us today? And more intriguingly, what can and must Christians today learn from both the Buddhist and the naturalist?

Scott Steinkerchner and Peter Hunter, both of the Order of Preachers (Dominicans), attempt to answer these questions in their *Pictures of the World: Three Views of Life, the Universe, and Everything*. The authors are not shy in delineating the universal scope of their reflections on the three aforementioned thinkers: As if "life" and "the universe" were not comprehensive enough, they add "everything" in their book's subtitle to make sure we don't miss the ambition of their work.

In three chapters the authors deftly and lucidly outline, in a very limited space and in an admirable economy of words, the basic thought-forms of Aquinas, Tsongkhapa, and Pinker. They have achieved this feat because they are not interested in expounding everything the three thinkers have said and the arguments they marshal to support their views but in depicting their *Pictures of the World*. A characteristic expression of the Austrian philosopher Ludwig Wittgenstein, "the picture of the world" or "world-picture" [*Weltbild*] refers not so much to specific beliefs as to the theoretical context and the overarching complex of patterns of inquiring and thinking within which individual convictions are obtained. To use another celebrated expression of Wittgenstein's, it is the game as such, with its own set of peculiar rules, and the players' skills in playing it, that we should take into consideration, and not a particular player's tactical moves, when we try to understand a match.

Placing these three "pictures of the world" in conversation with one another Steinkerchner and Hunter explore basic philosophical and theological issues such as the human person, the nature of reality and the way we know it, consciousness and free will, the divine act of creation, the basis of morality, gender equality, homosexuality and gay marriage, and stem-cell research. One salient feature of Steinkerchner's and Hunter's comparative analysis is their ability to bring the general patterns of thought of ancient thinkers such as Thomas Aquinas and Tsongkhapa to bear on controversial contemporary issues as well as to reveal the metaphysical roots of Pinker's anti-metaphysical stance.

Beside this insightful analysis of how these three epistemologically irreconcilable pictures of the world would approach today's hotly disputed metaphysical and ethical issues, Steinkerchner's and Hunter's major contribution is showcasing a new way of thinking and arguing about these red-hot problems of our time. Rather than forging a common viewpoint or arguing for the superiority of one viewpoint over the other two—both are impossible tasks—the authors demonstrate the possibility and necessity, persuasively to my mind, of a multi- and inter-epistemological approach. While Wittgenstein insists on identifying the one picture of the world of any thinker to grasp her many and diverse positions, today's context of religious pluralism requires us to cultivate the difficult but absolutely necessary skill to handle many—often conflicting—pictures of the world *at the same time and together*. Again, to put it in Wittgenstein's favorite metaphor, we must be able to play, possibly with equal skill, several games at the same time. In yet another metaphor, we must be able to play several musical instruments, ideally with equal competence. Indeed, it may be true that in our time to excel at one game or one musical instrument one needs to strengthen and improve one's skill at another game or musical instrument. The two authors have demonstrated just that kind of requisite multiple competence: they move with superb agility across three academic fields: Christian theology, Tibetan Buddhism, and philosophy of science.

FOREWORD

In religious living, to put the matter in a nutshell, to be religious today it is necessary to be so multireligiously and interreligiously. While Steinkerchner and Hunter may not favor this formula, their book opens the door for a challenging and fruitful conversation about mutual teaching and learning—on "life, the universe, and everything"—even among those who are ideologically far apart in these matters.

Introduction

What is the meaning of life, the universe, and everything? This humorously vague and expansive question of Douglas Adams from his *Hitchhiker's Guide to the Galaxy* is, nonetheless, something that many of us ponder throughout our lives—and none of us seem to get to the bottom of it. Does life have a meaning? Is love real? Is anything real? What does it mean to be human? How do we know? The problem with these questions is not that they have no answers, but that they have too many answers. Different people answer them differently, and how are we to know who is right or which answer is best? In Western society, these questions have traditionally been answered from within a Judeo-Christian world-picture. But since the Enlightenment, the traditional answers have been increasingly challenged by secular, scientific, and materialist viewpoints. More recently, the views of Eastern religions have also begun to make their mark in reframing some of these fundamental questions in the West.

We will explore the range of answers to these questions by painting three very different pictures of the world—Christian, Buddhist, and naturalist[1]—to see how the issues appear within each of them. To be able to say something true and useful, we will focus on one authority from within each of these traditions and give the answers from that perspective. Instead of trying to pin down how all Western religions see a particular point, for instance, we will focus on how one influential Christian theologian pictured it.

---

1. "Naturalism" is a loose term for philosophies built around the idea "that reality is exhausted by nature, containing nothing 'supernatural', and that the scientific method should be used to investigate all areas of reality, including the 'human spirit'" (Papineau, "Naturalism").

INTRODUCTION

After presenting Christian, Buddhist, and naturalist pictures of the world we will compare and contrast their views on a number of topics such as those mentioned above and more specialized questions such as what is consciousness, do we have free will, where did the universe come from, what is the basis of morality, and how to think about the morality of gender equality, gay marriage, and medical research involving embryonic stem cells? As a group, these questions cover the major areas of fundamental philosophy as well as display the diverse approaches our authors take in dealing with some controversial questions of today.

For Christianity we will focus on the thought of Thomas Aquinas (1225–74), a medieval theologian whose views are still considered authoritative within the Roman Catholic Church to this day. Aquinas read widely and integrated ideas from Judaism, Islam, and ancient Greek philosophy into his new synthesis of Christian thought. The fundamentals of his view involve an omnipotent God who creates the universe in order to share his love with humanity, remaining engaged with humanity in order to guide it to truth and happiness, ultimately in heaven. These ideas are shared broadly within various strands of Judaism, Islam, and Christianity.

For Buddhism we will focus on the thought of Tsong-kha-pa Blo-bzang-grags-pa (1357–1419), a religious reformer within Tibetan Buddhism whose views guide the largest Tibetan religious order, the Gelukpas, and whose thought is watched over by the head of the Gelukpa order, the Dalai Lama. Tsongkhapa created a new synthesis of individualistic/yogic and monastic/philosophical threads within Mahayana Buddhism to forge a system that advocates a slow, ethical, disciplined, philosophical path to break the beginningless cycle of reincarnation that all sentient beings suffer, while still allowing for immediate yogic enlightenment for advanced practitioners. Aspects of his views of the need for enlightenment to break the endless cycle of suffering called *samsara* and the validity of multiple paths to achieve that end are widely shared in other Buddhist and Hindu sects.

To represent the kind of naturalistic philosophy that has gained a credible voice in the West we will focus on the work of experimental psychologist Steven Pinker (b. 1954). Pinker's study of the evolutionary roots of language, logic, and morality have given him a full view of human nature that springs only from the potential within the natural realm, with no recourse to supernatural explanations. He regularly collaborates with such noted atheist scientists as Richard Dawkins, Sam Harris, and Daniel Dennett to guide public opinion toward understanding and accepting their

INTRODUCTION

vision and benefitting from their discoveries. Pinker's views on the origin of the universe, evolution, the nonexistence of the spiritual realm, and the primacy of the scientific method to establish truth claims have become mainstream in academic circles in the West.

These three pictures define different territories of possibilities. There is a divide between Eastern and Western religions on the relationship between rational and suprarational thought.[2] Eastern thought tends toward prioritizing suprarational above rational thought, marginalizing the role in logic in discovering the deepest truths about the world, while Western religions generally see logic as the primary arbiter of truth. This generally correlates with a Western penchant toward dogmatic statements that stand as markers of truth and an Eastern penchant for embracing contradictory statements as equally provisional expressions of ineffable truth. It also correlates with Western monotheism versus the embracing of multiple gods or multiple manifestations of the divine that is common in the East.

As we shall see, neither Aquinas nor Tsongkhapa lie at the ends of this pole, though the generalization still holds. Aquinas believes that rational thought can teach us truths about the world and about God, but these truths are never completely adequate to the reality of the divine, which can be touched more fully in a contemplative gaze. Aquinas laid down his pen after a mystical experience at the end of a long career of writing theology, saying, "I cannot do any more. Everything I have written seems to me as straw in comparison with what I have seen."[3] Tsongkhapa stresses the need for rational thought to cut through the delusions we have embraced about the world, though nothing ultimately true can be said with words or captured in the concepts they represent.

There is another territorial divide between embracing and denying transcendent reality—anything that exists above or beyond the natural bounds of the world of experience. Eastern and Western religions generally rely on the priority of an ultimate reality that is beyond the natural world and which holds the perfection of truth that is impossible to find in its purity in our ordinary experience of the physical world. Against this, naturalists hold that the natural realm is all that exists and disallows any explanatory power for supernatural realities. Words such as "meaning" and

---

2. "Suprarational" refers to ideas and ways of coming to knowledge that go beyond reason and rationality alone. It is not that these ideas would necessarily be in conflict with reason, but they could not be discovered or explained through reason alone.

3. Torrell, *Saint Thomas*, 289.

"ultimate truth" are generally seen as belonging to the transcendent realm, so naturalists tend to eschew any attribution of meaning to events beyond that which we ascribe to them for our own purposes, and tend to adjudicate truth claims pragmatically through the scientific method, with truth being defined as that which can best attain an agreed upon goal. There is no absolute, unchanging truth, just a series of provisionally adequate expressions that are held as true for a time. Against this, Eastern and Western religions tend to embrace guidance by absolute truths that humanity discovers rather than creates, and they search for the transcendent meaning behind mundane events. Absolute truth is always beyond the grasp of our minds while we are tied to this physical world, but it is ultimately what drives the world. Again, our paradigmatic thinkers do not lie at the extremes of this division, but they do embody it. The goal of Tsongkhapa's religious path is to allow an individual to glimpse ultimate truth, which is non-conceptual, but this is done through a careful and skeptical analysis of our real-world experiences. For Aquinas, God is absolutely transcendent and is truth itself, but God made the world, imbuing it with such essential meaning that even when it passes away, God will make a new world for us so that we can experience physical life forever. Pinker tries to expose and root out all recourses to transcendence in explaining the working of the world and the foundations of truth and morality, and he puts forward principles such as embracing human flourishing and avoiding suffering as if they were truths that had to be embraced by any right-thinking person.

The first three chapters of this book will deal with exploring the world-pictures of Aquinas, Tsongkhapa, and Pinker. Each will have their own chapter that will not be tied to the others so that they can each be seen on their own terms. The chapters are written as if the authors themselves were explaining their world-pictures, using their own phrases and examples as much as possible. References will be given as to where to find these arguments in the author's own works, but there are no narrative attributions such as, "According to Pinker . . ." Unless specified otherwise, if you are in chapter 3 all of the ideas come directly from Steven Pinker and word choices generally match his own.

A fourth chapter will compare them on the various topics noted above. In this chapter, we will also bring in new voices from each author's respective tradition in order to fill out the pictures on various topics. Aquinas, Tsongkhapa, and Pinker have given us well-thought-out pictures that touch on many topics, but they have not each commented directly on all of our topics, and in the case of Aquinas and Tsongkhapa, their traditions have continued to develop. Their faithful followers have a better insight into how they might have dealt with issues if they were still alive today than could be obtained by simply repeating their original words in this new context.

In the final chapter, we will explore what we might learn from studying other world-pictures. Specifically, since the authors of this book are both Catholic theologians in the line of Thomas Aquinas, we will show how we personally have been challenged to rethink Catholic beliefs and extend Aquinas's thought in light of what we have learned from Steven Pinker and Tsongkhapa and their respective traditions. Not that we have become Buddhists or naturalists, but we have benefitted from these inquiries and believe that they can point other Christians toward greater insight as well.

This last chapter also embodies our reason for writing this book. We hope to welcome readers into this rich discussion of the fundamental questions of life by showing just how far ranging the different views are on these various subjects. If you see yourself as belonging to one of these traditions or none of them, you can get a top-down view of what the world looks like from this perspective and a sensible explanation of why other people believe as they do about these topics. We hope to also challenge readers to become engaged in the discussion and use this information as a way to build out their own views on these subjects. By presenting some very different, very well-thought-out views on life, the universe, and everything, we implicitly ask the reader, "What do you think? What do you believe? What is your picture of the world and how does it differ from these? And most importantly, what can you learn from these other views?"

By referring to *world-pictures* and *pictures of the world* we are hearkening to the philosophy of Ludwig Wittgenstein, whose insight into how meaning is held and communicated informs our approach. A reader need not know the philosophy of Wittgenstein to read this book, but it greatly informs our method of writing it. Wittgenstein pointed out that investigating a question implies that one has a context for answering it that has to include many things outside the immediate scope of inquiry, such as what counts for evidence and what we already assume to be true. If we tried to question *everything* at once we would have no basis on which to resolve the issue.[4] But the context that provides the framework for our questioning is not so much a series of specific beliefs as it is a picture we hold in our minds about how it all fits together. Hence, Wittgenstein refers to a

4. Wittgenstein, *On Certainty*, § 337–43.

world-picture (*Weltbild*) rather than a *worldview* (*Weltanschauung*). As an example, Wittgenstein notes that we moderns hold a picture of the Earth as a round ball floating in space, and we employ that picture when we go to make a bridge, deciding to build it in one place or the other, and how large the beams need to be.[5] Wittgenstein usually refers to *world-picture* in the singular, referring to one, overarching picture that governs all of our thinking and inquiring. One of the authors of this book, Scott Steinkerchner, has argued that people do not typically operate with one overarching world-picture, but instead have several world-pictures that they employ in different areas of their life without ever reconciling these into a larger whole—perhaps employing one world-picture in their professional work and a different one in their personal interactions.[6] The learning that comes through interreligious dialogue relies on our natural ability to work with multiple world-pictures. New insights are gained as we learn to see the world through this other world-picture and then reflect on the ways it fits and doesn't with our own picture.

This is the kind of learning we are hoping to foster by painting for our readers three quite different world-pictures. The great thinkers we are investigating here have worked to expand and integrate their own world-pictures so that they can make universal comments that apply across disparate parts of our lives, personal and public. In order to highlight the pictures themselves we will not delve into all of the reasons these authors give as to why they believe their pictures are true. This sort of information will only appear if it helps explain what is really meant. These chapters are not apologetics for belief, they are descriptions of each of these author's picture of the world that guides their thinking and writing about it, and through them, guides the thought of millions of others.

---

5. Wittgenstein, *On Certainty*, § 146–48.
6. Steinkerchner, *Beyond Agreement*, 49.

1

Thomas Aquinas
A Christian Picture of the World

Twelfth and thirteenth-century Europe experienced a period of relative peace and prosperity that allowed it to become a hotbed of creativity and achievement.[1] Benedictine Abbot Suger rejuvenated sacred architecture through the invention of the Gothic style of architecture when he rebuilt the eastern end of his church at the Abbey of Saint-Denis in the outskirts of Paris from 1140 to 1144. The older Romanesque style had relied on rounded arches that required thick, sturdy walls and columns to support the outward thrust they generate. His Gothic architecture used pointed arches that alleviated the outward thrust, allowing thinner walls and columns for support, leaving space for windows to dominate the walls rather than stone. Subsequently, between 1180 and 1270 the people of France, with a population of just eighteen million, built eighty cathedral-sized churches and six hundred abbeys.[2]

---

1. Cultural context based on O'Meara, "Paris," 695–704.
2. O'Meara, "Paris," 696.

Figure 1.1: *Sainte Chapelle*, Paris, France.

These cathedrals, with their thin columns, high vaulting, and large windows gave people the experience of a transcendent God of light. Their overall designs with complex elements of stained glass, stone carvings, sacred furnishings, pillars, and ribs all perfectly ordered toward a single, transcendent purpose, spoke of a universe of diversity that was all part of God's one grand design.

At the same time, the intellectual life of Europe was advancing through the rediscovery of Greek philosophy and the translation of the works of Aristotle into Latin, initially from Arabic, as the Muslim world had kept alive the thought of Aristotle, and later from Greek directly. This fueled a reworking of philosophy and theology that led to the creation of universities in Oxford, Paris, and Bologna and the rise of Scholasticism. Scholars such as Albert the Great and Roger Bacon placed a new emphasis on the study of the natural world, leading eventually to the creation of modern science. While theologians such as Bonaventure argued in favor of holding closely to the Neo-Platonic philosophy that had guided Augustine in the fifth century, Thomas Aquinas embraced many of the newly rediscovered views of Aristotle, creating a new synthesis of Christian philosophy. Aquinas's view eventually became more popular in the Roman Catholic Church and, while not every view of Aquinas's is still held, to this day his synthesis is given pride of place in theological education.

Aquinas pioneered a new form of theological writing, the *Summa Theologiae*.[3] The standard framework used to teach theology in Aquinas's day was Peter Lombard's *Sentences*, a collection of quotes taken from various church documents and the fathers of the church, loosely arranged into subject areas. New master theologians would typically write their own commentary on the *Sentences* as well as commentaries on various books of the Bible and then teach from these. Aquinas recognized the shortcomings of this approach as topics could only be treated as they came up in these texts, allowing for many omissions and needless repetitions. He wrote his *Summa Theologiae* as a textbook to guide new students through the entirety of theology in a way that was pedagogically effective. It comprehensively dealt with the entirety of theology as an organic whole, arranging the material in a way that highlighted the inherent internal connections as one idea built upon another. Others followed in his footsteps, and summas[4] multiplied, replacing the *Sentences* as primary textbooks. Though it was never finished, Aquinas's *Summa* is the best place to look to find his ideas on most theological topics.

Gothic cathedrals, in one important respect, shared the same goal as Aquinas's *Summa*—to show a "harmony out of diversity, order within variety."[5] Both cathedrals and summas sought to convey a vision of a greater, overarching, transcendent reality by arranging their particular elements within a greater unity that revealed the larger truth through attention to the details of individual truths and the connections between

---

3. Context and motivations for writing the *Summa* from Torrell, *Saint Thomas*, 1:142–48.

4. The Latin word *"summa"* means "summary."

5. O'Meara, "Paris," 702.

them. Individual elements of art within a cathedral and individual questions within the *Summa* have a truth of their own, a message to convey. But the work as a whole unites and arranges the elements into a larger truth, placing various elements in interpretive juxtaposition to other elements to tell this larger story.

A Picture

Figure 1.2: The interior apse of Sainte Chapelle, in which was housed Jesus's crown of thorns, a classic of Gothic architecture.

To help to understand Aquinas's picture of the world, let's turn to a classic of Gothic architecture, Sainte Chapelle, on the *Ile de la Cité*, an island in the river Seine in Paris, France. It is pictured in figures 1.1, 1.2, and 1.3. Sainte Chapelle was built not as a cathedral but rather as a private chapel for King Louis IX to house twenty-two holy relics, most notably the crown of thorns worn by Jesus to his crucifixion.[6] It was completed while Aquinas was a student in Paris just opposite the island on the left bank of the river. Aquinas

---

6. O'Meara, "Paris," 697–98. Jesus Christ, from whom Christianity takes its name, was tortured and condemned to death by crucifixion, being nailed to a wooden cross. One of the tortures he suffered before his death was having a crown made of large thorns placed on his head because he had been controversially proclaimed to be the king of the Jewish people.

would later return to the University of Paris as a master theologian and Louis IX became his patron, financing his personal secretaries, so it not difficult to imagine Aquinas occasionally visiting this holy place.

The windows in Sainte Chapelle are not simply impressive. It is as if the walls themselves are made of light. Scenes of prophets and kings and queens from the Hebrew Bible fill the stained glass in the main body of the church, along with an entire window dedicated just to the history of the relics contained in the chapel. In the apse surrounding the reliquary holding the Crown of Thorns are scenes from the life of Christ. The stained glass scenes reaching back across time present their stories not to be read, but to be entered into by stepping into their light. Together the stories lead up to and away from the story of the greatest prophet and king who had worn this very crown to his death on the cross. While the images are of old, they connect King Louis IX to the line of ancient Jewish kings and to the protection of the story of Jesus, thus religiously enhancing his prestige.

The details of all of these stories are portrayed in vivid detail, but the effect is to draw one into the light that shines through the windows, uniting the chapel as one larger story told throughout the generations.

Figure 1.3: Interior of Sainte Chapelle, showing tourists lost in its beauty.

As one gazes at the windows, one is drawn to see the light above and beyond them, the light that makes all of this possible, the light that shines through these stories and envelopes the worshipper and the holy relic in one embrace. The chapel as a whole represents the world graced by God throughout history. This is the same mundane world that exists outside the chapel, but inside the chapel the world is iconized such that one can see its fundamental connection to God. The windows contain scenes from the Christian tradition showing how God has carefully worked with his people over the course of history to lead them to where they are now. The windows do not shine of their own accord. As the sun shines through the windows, the grace of God shines through prophets, kings and queens, and holy relics of old, bringing grace to humanity. An observer is drawn to see the grace of God shining through a particular saint or prophet as an icon of God's grace shining through the entire created order that surrounds us, drawing us all up into the life of God so that we might merge with that great light. The chapel as a whole represents the grace of God working throughout history to make God's people holy and invite them into the light that embraces all. This was one of Aquinas's goals in writing his *Summa* as well.[7]

God created the world. God is a not a part of the world and the world is not a part of God. God stands apart from the world as its source. God is all-good, all-love, and all-truth, and God created the world in order to share this goodness, love, and truth, and so the world is fundamentally good and loved and knowable. Humanity, the summit of material creation, is fashioned in the image of God with the ability to know and to love, so that we might know and love God back, thus obtaining our greatest joy. Unfortunately, the first humans ruined the delicate harmony that God had placed within them, corrupting themselves by losing this integration, and then because they no longer were integrated, they were incapable of passing that harmony on to their posterity. This state of corruption is called "original sin." We are fundamentally good, known, and loved by God and created to know and love all that is good, but we are not able to achieve our full potential because of our brokenness. God does not abandon us in this broken state, and has worked not only to heal us but to raise us up to a

---

7. Aquinas, *Summa Theologiae*, 1:2.1. Rather than page numbers, it is standard practice to refer to passages in the *Summa Theologiae* by book, questions, and article. The preceding reference is thus to the first book, question 2, article 1. If the citation refers to the main text of the answer, the reference is complete. Sometimes the citation will refer to Aquinas's response to one of the objections rather than to the main text, and that will be noted as "resp." followed by the response number.

greater state than our natures would allow if we had never been corrupted. To understand this, we need to go back and look more carefully at each of the steps we have just outlined.

The Nature of God

God created the world, but God was not created.[8] God is self-existing. God's very nature is to exist. In Aquinas's language, God is "existence itself." God exists independently of space and time, because space and time are part of created reality (and God is uncreated).

You and I exist, or at least I existed when I wrote this and you exist when you are reading it. Perhaps you are reading this years after I have written it and you do not exist yet as I write these lines. As human beings, there is a difference between us and our existence. I can think about you, the reader, and then wonder if you exist. In the same way we could discuss separately what unicorns are and whether or not they exist. This is not true about God. As existence itself, it makes no sense to try to establish what God is and then inquire as to whether or not God exists. Existence is something we have, but it is what God is.

Unlike you and I, there was no time in the past when God did not exist nor could there be a time in the future when God would cease to exist. That would be impossible. Yet God does not exist in time and God is not one of the things that exist in this world. God's existence is apart from time and apart from the world. We know that there was a beginning to the world because God had revealed this to be the case, but it is logically possible that the world had no beginning in time, as it is logically possible that the world has no end in time and will continue on forever. But even if this were the case, there would still be a difference between what the world is and the world's existence. The world is not its own existence. To exist, the world relies on existence itself, God. You and I, time and the world have existence. God is existence itself. Only God exists necessarily. You and I might not have existed. You and I came to exist at some point. God has always existed. Even if the world did not come to exist at some time, if it extended infinitely backwards in time, it would still owe its existence to God.

As pure existence, nothing in God passes away or comes to be over time. God cannot change, improve, or evolve. God is God's own eternity.

8. This section relates some of the major points of Aquinas's Treatise on the One God in Aquinas, *Summa Theologiae*, 1:2–26.

God is truth itself and is omnipotent, so God's omnipotence does not include the ability to do things that are logically impossible, such as to change the past, or to change or to contradict himself.[9] Being outside of time, God can equally see all things, past and future—what was, what is, what will be, and what could be but never will.

There can only be one thing that is existence itself and is the basis for all that exists, or there would be two existences, everything that "exists" and "everything else that does not exist but does something like existing," which makes no sense. So existence is one, and God is one. But God is one as a Trinity of persons: Father, Son, and Holy Spirit.[10] Reason does not tell us that this is so, God has revealed it. To be true to reason and revelation, these could not be three persons who come together to become one God, nor could they simply be different manifestations of the one God. Revelation tells us that he Father is the source. The Son is the perfect image of the Father, containing everything of the Father, and so equally God. The Spirit is the love that binds the Father and the Son, which is so complete as to be equal to all that they are, and thus equally God. While understanding this completely is beyond our ability, an analogy can help. The Son is like the perfect thought of the Father, a Word spoken that contains everything the Father is and so is just like the Father, except that the Father is the thinker and the Son is the thought, or the Father the speaker and the Son the Word, the Father the generator and the Son generated. This generation is eternal, as God exists outside of time. The Son is not outside the Father, as a thought is not outside the thinker. In addition, goodness that is known is loved, and the Father loves the Son and the Son loves the Father and this complete love that binds them is the Spirit.

Creation and Meaning

God lacks nothing. But in this perfect existence God wished to share God's perfect love, and so God created the world.[11] The world shares in

9. Aquinas also held that God could not create formless matter, something that was nothing, since this was logically impossible (Aquinas, *Summa Theologiae*, 1:66.1). This position was controversial, as Aquinas acknowledges, since the Bible's book of Genesis opens with God hovering over what could be construed as formless matter. Aquinas's opinion was condemned as heretical after his death (Turner, *Thomas Aquinas*, 49–50).

10. This section relates some of the major points of Aquinas's Treatise on the Trinity in Aquinas, *Summa Theologiae*, 1:27–43.

11. Aquinas, *Summa Theologiae*, 1:47.1.

the very being of God. It is created by the entire Trinity rather than any single person of the Trinity.[12] God created the world as an artist creates a piece of art—intentionally, with knowledge and will.[13] Each person of the Trinity has a proper role in creation.[14] The Father creates through the word conceived in his mind, which is the Son, and according to his love for what is created, which is the Holy Spirit. In fact, God revealed the divine persons so that we would know that God created us not out of necessity but through the love of God's own goodness, and thus we would know how to live rightly in love.[15]

All things that exist get their existence from God not only when they are created, but as long as they are preserved in existence, as the day lasts only as long as the sun keeps lighting up the sky, or as a song exists as long as its singer sings.[16] Thus, God is at the core of all things that exist, and all things that exist reflect God's being. Things that are living manifest an even greater likeness to God through their activity.[17] Intelligent life reflects God to an even greater degree than other things, since intelligent life can know and love and act on its own decisions. Thus, we say that humanity was made in the image of God. God created the world out of love, and the world is most fulfilled when it returns to God in love. The material world does best through human beings, intellectual animals, and so they are the capstone of material creation.[18]

The Nature of Things

Picture the world full of individual things with fixed natures, each one in some way created by God in accord with a master plan.[19] Things can change, but only in certain ways and not others, governed by their nature.[20]

12. Aquinas, *Summa Theologiae*, 1:45.6.
13. Aquinas, *Summa Theologiae*, 1:44.3.
14. Aquinas, *Summa Theologiae*, 1:45.6.
15. Aquinas, *Summa Theologiae*, 1:32.1 resp. 3.
16. Aquinas, *Summa Theologiae*, 1:8.1.
17. Aquinas, *Summa Theologiae*, 1:93.2.
18. Aquinas thought, however, that there were immaterial creatures, pure spirits, which he identifies with the angels and demons of Scripture. They, not us, are the pinnacle of the whole of creation, material and spiritual (Aquinas, *Summa Theologiae*, 1:89.1).
19. Aquinas, *Summa Theologiae*, 1:47.1.
20. Aquinas, *Summa Theologiae*, 1:105.6.

An acorn can potentially become an oak tree, but it cannot become a cherry tree nor a lump of gold. God does not govern all the changes in the world directly, they are governed by the natures that God gave them and by their interaction with other things. The nature of an acorn includes the potential to become an oak tree and not any other kind of tree, but in order to grow it also relies on a number of other things as well, such as water, soil, sunlight, and time. All acorns have the potential to become oaks, even though few of them actually grow to maturity, because they all share in acorn nature. This is not to say there is a single "nature of acorns" that subsists somewhere that each particular acorn taps into. Individual acorns exist, and each one is governed by its own individual nature. However, acorns are such that their individual natures are the same in many respects, which is why they are all really acorns. Whether or not a particular acorn grows into an oak depends on its complex interactions with other things around it, with each one being governed by its own individual nature. There is no external control. Things in this world act and interact with their environment guided by their own internal nature rather than by some external guiding force. God intentionally created the world this way, and so everything in the world is in some sense under God's control.

In becoming an oak, an acorn would cease being an acorn and would take on a new nature, the nature of an oak.[21] The oak could continually undergo a series of smaller changes without ceasing to be an oak—growing taller, getting and losing leaves as seasons pass, etc. The nature of being an oak includes these sorts of smaller changes. Eventually, the oak might die or be cut down and sawed into lumber. This would again be a change in its nature, and these changes would be made possible by the nature of oak trees: it's part of the nature of an oak that it can die and become lumber.

The form or individual nature that governs something that exists in its own right—allowing it to exist on its own rather than being dependent upon something else and making it one thing with particular properties—is called a *substantial* form. If a thing is alive, its substantial form is called a *soul*. Acorns and oaks have souls; lumber is made out of wood, which has a substantial form that is not a soul. Living things exhibit a unity that non-living things do not. Living things grow and respond to their environment, seeking to preserve themselves in existence, and they create offspring that are like themselves. The abilities of different living things differ greatly,

---

21. For an explanation of substance, accident, and change see Aquinas, *On Being and Essence*. For a longer explanation, see Brower, *Aquinas's Ontology*.

and so they thrive in very different environments. Fish have gills, which let them breathe under water. Birds have wings so that they can fly. Humans have neither gills nor wings, but they have two spiritual qualities, intelligence and will, allowing them to thrive in ways that other animals cannot.

Intelligence and Will

Intelligence is the ability to understand the world through grasping general principles and reasoning about them.[22] General principles are learned from our experiences of the world and through communicating with others. All animals, including ourselves, sense the world and have an ability to understand the world at the level of sensation. Most can navigate their environment and recognize and selectively take in food. Some animals even have natural instincts to do complex tasks such as building nests or migrating according to the season. Beyond these abilities, humans can think about the future, their needs, the usefulness of materials, and the habits of their prey.[23] While brute animals build nests and migrate in fixed patterns, depending upon the species, intelligent animals such as humans can adapt and build different homes suitable to a wide range of environments, taking clues from other animals if we choose, and migrating because of a conscious decision.

Intelligent animals like us can do this because we have the ability to derive general principles from our sense data, understand the nature of things, share this understanding with others, and employ our understanding in reasoning about future situations. We can experience the changing of the seasons and know that the weather will turn cold for the next four months, and we can make a decision about building a warmer house or moving to a warmer climate for that period. We could see that acorns fall from oak trees, watch some of them sprout and others not, and understand

---

22. The basics of Aquinas's view of how we come to know the things of our world are found in Aquinas, *Summa Theologiae*, 1:84–87.

23. Modern science is studying the intelligence of various animals and there are indications that some birds, dolphins, apes, and monkeys have the capacity for conceptual thinking and abstract reasoning. Aquinas did not believe that any non-human animals had these abilities, and most modern Thomists have been reticent to contradict this opinion. The argument here is what the ability to do abstract reasoning indicates about human nature. If some day the consensus opinion is that other animals are also intelligent, we would not have to reevaluate human nature, but would have to conclude that these other animals also share in the aspects of human nature that are concomitant with intelligence.

that given the right environment acorns grow into oaks. We can see a log and understand how it might make a good beam for the roof of our house, especially if we saw off the extraneous parts.

In coming to know the nature of oak trees we take something of them into ourselves, but the nature of oak must exist in us in a different mode than it does in the oak.[24] If we are to say that we know oak trees, our knowledge must have come from them. Our knowledge could be secondhand, derived from the knowledge of others who have told us about oaks, but let us explore what it means to come to know real, living oak trees through our own experience of them.

Oaks are subsistent living things composed of both a form and matter.[25] It is the oak, composed of form and matter, that exists in its own right. Neither the oak's form nor its matter exist in their own right. They exist as parts of the oak, and they derive their existence from it.

The nature or essence of oaks is what belongs to all oaks by necessity in that they are oaks. Oak nature cannot include having ten branches, because some oaks have more and some less, but it would include having branches. Oak nature is not essentially one or many—one and many are beyond the nature of oak. If oak nature were one, it could not be made plural by existing in numerous individual oaks. If oak nature were by nature many, it could not exist as it does in a single oak. Oak nature has a double existence.[26] It exists as essentially individual in individual oaks and then

---

24. This explanation of what it means to know is directly from Aquinas, *On Being and Essence*.

25. *Subsistent* here means that they actually exist in the world, not simply in our minds. The forms of oaks are called *substantial* because by it the oaks actually exist in the world as real live oaks. Their substantial forms are called *souls* because they are living. But for simplicity's sake, we will not use that terminology in the arguments that follow.

26. This is a paraphrase of a crucial section that reads: "The nature considered in this way, however, has a double existence. It exists in singulars on the one hand, and in the soul on the other, and from each of these there follow accidents. In singulars, furthermore, the essence has a multiple existence according to the multiplicity of singulars. Nevertheless, if we consider the essence in the first, or absolute, sense, none of these pertain to the essence. For it is false to say that the essence of man, considered absolutely, has existence in this singular, because if existence in this singular pertained to man insofar as he is man, man would never exist outside this singular. Similarly, if it pertained to man insofar as he is man not to exist in this singular, then the essence would never exist in the singular. But it is true to say that man, but not insofar as he is man, has whatever may be in this singular or in that one, or else in the soul. Therefore, the nature of man considered absolutely abstracts from every existence, though it does not exclude the existence of anything either. And the nature thus considered is the one predicated of each individual."

becomes plural through the multiplicity of oaks. But oak nature, as understood by us, does not exist in any single oak, or it could not exist outside of that oak. At the same time, if oak nature was understood by us as not existing in any single oak tree, then it could not be the essence of any single oak, and we would not know oaks.

For these reasons, we see that oak nature exists in us differently than it exists in oaks. The nature of oaks as understood by us abstracts from every existence while not excluding them, and the nature thus considered is predicated of the individual oaks. Our understanding of oaks, abstracted from individuals, is related uniformly to all oaks, applying equally to each insofar as it is an oak. But oak nature exists differently in oaks. It is always individuated. Our intellect attributes universality to the nature of oak—that oak nature applies not just for us with particular oaks at particular times, but for all oaks and people at all times—not because oak nature exists in oaks as a universal, nor because of the way oak nature exists in our intellect, but because of its relation to oaks as their likeness.

What is true for our knowledge of oaks is true for our knowledge of anything composed of matter and form, which is everything physical that exists in the world. "Forms are not actually intelligible except as they are separated from matter and its conditions, and forms are not made actually intelligible except by virtue of an intelligent substance, which educes the forms and receives them in itself." Knowledge is necessarily immaterial. We, as knowing subjects, must have an active immaterial part of ourselves that can separate the formal from the material principles in the objects we encounter, and we must have a passive immaterial part of ourselves to hold these abstracted forms.

The immateriality of knowledge can also be seen in our ability to know all of material reality without exception.[27] If our knowledge were material in nature, the specifics of its materiality would impose limitations and mask our ability to know some things in something like the way our hearing would be impaired if our ears made a noise. This does not happen, so our knowing faculty must subsist on an immaterial level, unbounded by material constraints. Our learning can be bounded by material constraints, because it intrinsically involves a connection to the material world, but not our knowing. Ideas such as "human rights" are by nature immaterial, but the idea of "human rights" is not subsistent—it does not actually exist on its own. It exists in minds. People, however, must exist substantially to be

---

27. Aquinas, *Summa Theologiae*, 1:75.2.

able to know ideas such as "human rights." To be free from all limitations, our knowing cannot rely on a material organ, or it would be conditioned by the physical limitations of that organ, in the same way that looking through tinted glass would affect our ability to see colors.

Reasoning is the process of coming to new conclusions based on ideas we already have (premises) and using certain patterns of inference. For example, if I know that humans are animals, and I know that all animals grow old and die, I can come to know that all humans grow old and die by reasoning from those premises to this conclusion. Most premises are themselves the result of reasoning, or they come from our experience of the world, but some are known immediately. They are the kind of claims that, when we consider them, we realize must be true. Very important among these, it is immediately knowable that existence and nonexistence are mutually exclusive. Nothing can exist and not exist at the same time and in the same respect. I exist, and there was a time when I did not exist, but at no time did I both exist and not exist. Truth expresses what is, falsity expresses what is not, and so truth and falsity are also mutually exclusive. This is called the Law of Noncontradiction.

We also have a power called our will, which is at its center a capacity for desire, a capacity to desire what we understand as in some ways good for us. Human beings have a natural, general inclination toward what is perceived as good.[28] We can desire things that are actually bad for us, but only by seeing them as good in some way. A diabetic may desire chocolate, which is very bad for her, but only because the chocolate is also good, as its sweet taste is enjoyable.

Because I can understand the world in indefinitely many ways, I can desire it in indefinitely many ways. Created things are good, but they are good for me in some respects and bad for me in others. I can think of a juicy steak as delicious and full of protein, or I can think of it as produced in a meat industry I don't agree with, or high in cholesterol. Some of those ways of thinking about the steak make it attractive, good to eat, and some of those ways make me want to avoid eating it—and because I can weigh those different ways of seeing the steak according to how they matter to me, I can choose whether to eat it or not.

The will is free, because it is not determined by its object. The steak does not make me want to eat it. The things we desire are good in some ways and bad in others, so we desire them (or not) according to our own

---

28. Aquinas, *Summa Theologiae*, 1:79.12.

criteria and knowledge about them. Our will is not determined from outside ourselves and we are not forced into making certain choices and not others, though some things are very hard for anyone to resist. Just as God does not make everything happen directly, but gives created things their own natures by which they interact with the rest of the world, so God doesn't determine our wills. We act in genuine freedom.[29]

The other animals—as flexible and powerful as their sensual grasp of the world is, and their desires that follow on that understanding—lack the abstract, universal understanding that humans have, and consequently lack will, in this full sense of a desire following on that special, universal kind of understanding. When our next-door neighbor shouts at a cat for catching birds and calls it a bad cat, we find it faintly amusing, because catching birds is just in a cat's nature. The cat cannot learn why it might want to transcend its natural desire and become a vegetarian, but people can.

The Good Life

God is in all things that exist as the cause of their very existence, and all creation can enjoy the love of God at some level by existing and embodying its nature. God exists in intelligent creatures in another mode as well—by being known and loved. *Intelligent* here is being used in its fullest sense of personal beings that can understand abstract ideas, make free choices, and love. Only intelligent creatures can come to know and understand God's love for them and can choose to respond by loving God in return, thus more fully entering into the divine joy. In this way, intelligent creatures are the capstone of creation.

Since humans have a free will, individuals set their own goals and direct their own actions in trying to achieve them. Working toward one's goals brings joy and a sense of meaning to life, but there are various degrees of joy and meaning, and many factors contribute to how much joy and meaning people find in their lives. God has given intelligent animals understanding, reason, and will in order to share more fully in the goodness, joy, and love of God, and so they naturally find joy in exercising these faculties.

To live a good life we also need to learn about the world we live in and how it functions and take this into account in our choices. For instance, we can see that, in general, parents love their children and take care of them. When we reflect on this, we can understand that this is the way the world

29. Aquinas, *Summa Theologiae*, 1:83.1.

is supposed to function or else children, who are naturally helpless, would never be able to survive infancy. Thus, we commit ourselves to taking care of the needs of our own children, and when we encounter parents with no regard for their young children, we don't see that as a neutral fact but as problematic. Our analysis of the natural world provides some moral demands called the "natural law," which are, as the example of child-rearing makes clear, simply an expression of what leads to human flourishing. Acting in accord with the natural law leads to better lives for all.

People are inherently social. We accomplish more and find joy and meaning through interactions with others. Our goals and actions should reflect this and help to build up the well-being of the society around us.

Human beings are always changing.[30] As we learn more, we can better discern how to act and are better able to love. At birth, human beings have enormous potential, but it takes a lifetime to actualize that potential.

Some goals when realized bring great amounts of joy, while others can leave us feeling empty, so if we want to have a good life we must learn about life and the world in order to be able to choose better goals for ourselves. One of the best ways to choose long-term goals is to look at others who have gone before and lived lives that we judge to be successful and learn the goals that guided their lives.

Original Sin

As we see what brings joy and meaning to life, we realize that people's actions often lead away from joy toward pain and suffering. Though people always act for what they perceive to be best at the moment, they do not always actually act in their own best interest. Indeed, it often seems that a lot of what humans do makes their own lives and the lives of others harder and more miserable, and not happier. This is caused by many factors, but overall it is because our desires conflict with one another and are out of line with what is truly best for us. This condition is called original sin, and it gives all people a proclivity toward sinning, acting against their own best interest and against the best interests of others. At the beginning of time, God gave us a special help to keep our desires aligned with what was truly

---

30. Torrell, *Saint Thomas*, 2:306: "According to Thomas, nature is a dynamic, not a static, reality. It is therefore not entirely itself except when it is cultivated. Natural man is not man in a brutish or savage state, but the man who is fulfilled in accord with the main inclinations of his nature in search of the true and the good in all their forms."

best for us, a condition called original justice. But the first humans, Adam and Eve, chose to act against their own good, and in doing so lost original justice, and consequently could not hand it on to us, their descendants.

This teaching explains a fact about ourselves, our tendency to choose against our own best interests, and reconciles that fact with the belief that God made us good.

Life After Life in Heaven

God made the world in order to share the divine love and goodness, so God planned from the beginning to remedy the situation of original sin.[31] God is the greatest truth and the one most worthy of our love, so people find their ultimate fulfillment in knowing and loving God.[32] However, this is impossible in this world where we do not see God directly.[33] In this life, we only see God's effects upon the world. Since we cannot find our ultimate fulfillment here in this life, God invites us into a new life in heaven where we will see God face to face and all our pain and sin will be no more. Heaven is the culmination of our existence. It fulfills our nature, it does not abnegate it, though by nature we do not have the ability to live in heaven.[34] God had to give us grace, a share in his own divine life, raising us above our natural state, for us to live in heaven. Just as we have bodies here in this world, we will have bodies in heaven.[35] However, our bodies in heaven will be perfect, free from all pain and sorrow, and incorruptible, and so our bodies will be different in heaven than they are now.[36] Our wills will also no longer be divided in heaven, so original sin will be healed and we will love only what is truly good and right.

The Need for Religion

Human beings do not have the natural ability to get to heaven so God gives them help to achieve this ultimate end. Because of original sin, human

---

31. Torrell, *Saint Thomas*, 2:110–12.
32. Aquinas, *Summa Theologiae*, 1–2.1.8.
33. Aquinas, *Summa Theologiae*, 1:88.3.
34. Aquinas, *Summa Theologiae*, 1–2:5.5.
35. Aquinas, *Summa Theologiae*, Supplement:75.1.
36. Aquinas, *Summa Theologiae*, Supplement:82.1–2.

beings do not even have the ability to maximize their natural potential in this life, and so again, God provides divine help. Help from God is called grace. Grace comes in many forms. God chose the Jewish people, the descendants of Abraham, to receive his revelation and be his chosen people, giving them their own law through Moses and periodically sending them prophets. God rescued them from slavery in Egypt and settled them in their own land so that they could live according to his law.

God augmented human understanding with the revelation in the form of the law and the prophets because our happiness relies on our own reason and knowledge and that reasoning and knowledge can sometimes be flawed.[37] Revelation tells us things that are important for living right that we might not otherwise know. Revelation makes up for the fact that human reasoning can have errors, and that not everyone has the time or ability to figure out the most important truths about how to live well. Revelation helps us live better by augmenting our own search for truth. Authentic revelation can never contradict correct reasoning since God is truth itself, made the world, and gave us reason in order that we might know the world and thus live rightly. Though, because of our finite abilities, we can never completely know truth the way God does. For instance, through revelation we can come to know that the one God exists as a Trinity of persons who freely created the world out of overflowing love. This can teach us that the world is fundamentally good and that we are meant to love one another and to love God, but only God can fully understand what it means to be a Trinity of persons. We can know something about it, but we cannot understand it completely.

As the final remedy for original sin, God sent his only son Jesus into the world as the final, definitive revelation. Jesus, the eternal second person of the Trinity and Word of God, became human, taking on a human nature by being conceived by the power of the Holy Spirit in the Virgin Mary (without a human father). Jesus grew up and began teaching, gathering a group of disciples, was killed through a collusion of Jewish and Roman authorities by being nailed to a cross, rose from the dead, and ascended into heaven. God then sent the Holy Spirit upon the community of his followers, empowering them to carry on Jesus's saving work and transforming them into the church, the mystical body of Christ here on earth. The church carries on the work of salvation by proclaiming his message to the world

---

37. Aquinas, *Summa Theologiae*, 1:1.1.

in word and action and to administer God's grace by performing the sacraments Jesus prescribed.

Jesus's life, death, and resurrection was so powerful that it did not simply reverse the effects of original sin: it opened for humanity the chance to live with God in heaven. In the life, actions, and words of Jesus humanity finds the fullness of revelation, the definitive expression of God's plan for the world. Also, by coming to know and love God incarnate in Jesus, whom we can see, we are led to know and love more the God we cannot see.[38] By joining human and divine nature in the person of Jesus, God gives us hope that we might be joined to the divine nature in heaven.[39] By Jesus's total submission to the will of the Father and, though innocent, going willingly to his death on the cross, he gained an infinite amount of merit. This power is manifested in his own resurrection to new life. Rather than simply being resuscitated back to this life, the resurrection of Jesus shows us that we too might be given a new life in God. There is sufficient merit in Jesus's death and resurrection to save the whole world, allowing everyone to join God in heaven.[40] But God would not force salvation on anyone, so first this salvation goes to those of his followers whose words, thoughts, and actions show that they want it. To assist in the distribution of grace, Jesus left the church seven sacraments that confer specific sharings in this grace. A sacrament is a specific ritual involving words and actions that confers a specific grace upon the recipient. The first of these sacraments to be given anyone is baptism, by which the Holy Spirit enters them, erasing original sin and entering them into a new life of grace.[41] Baptism also opens for us the gates of heaven[42] and makes us part of the mystical body of Christ, which is the church.[43] The salvation gained by Jesus naturally belongs to anyone who is joined to his mystical body, as salvation won by someone's hands would make up for a sin committed by the person's feet.[44]

---

38. Aquinas, *Summa Theologiae*, 2–2:83.3 resp. 2.

39. See Torrell, *Saint Thomas*, 2:111, where he quotes *Compendium of Theology* 1:201.

40. Aquinas, *Summa Theologiae*, 3:8.3 resp. 1: "Ad primum ergo dicendum quod illi qui sunt infideles, etsi actu non sint de Ecclesia, sunt tamen in potentia. Quae quidem potentia in duobus fundatur, primo quidem et principaliter, in virtute Christi, quae sufficiens est ad salutem totius humani generis; secundario, in arbitrii libertate."

41. Aquinas, *Summa Theologiae*, 1–2:81.3 resp. 1.

42. Aquinas, *Summa Theologiae*, 1:74.3 resp. 4.

43. Aquinas, *Summa Theologiae*, 1–2:5.7 resp. 2.

44. Aquinas, *Summa Theologiae*, 3:49.1.

Aquinas and the Christian Tradition

Like others of his day, Thomas Aquinas worked to create a new synthesis of Christian thought that would bind its various elements together so that one could see the forest for the trees. His approach wedded ideas from the newly rediscovered pagan philosopher Aristotle, recovered through the hands of Muslim scholars, to traditional Christian beliefs that had been heavily influenced by neo-Platonic thought for centuries. As one might imagine, his views were controversial and not universally accepted. Even members of his own religious order, the Dominicans, were inclined to think he was too radical in his acceptance of much of Aristotle's philosophy. Many theologians, the Franciscan scholar Bonaventure, for example, or the Dominican Archbishop of Canterbury, Richard Kilwardby, thought a more traditional Augustinian, neo-Platonic theology should endure. On the other side, radical Aristotelians, or Averroists,[45] as they were sometimes called, thought Aquinas hadn't gone far enough, and should be willing to throw out Christian doctrines in response to Aristotle's arguments.[46]

Three years after Aquinas's death, Kilwardby and the bishop of Paris, Steven Tempier, each published a list of theological proposition that they condemned as heretical, which included ideas manifestly supported by Aquinas.[47] Despite this, Aquinas's views began gaining ground and he became a trophy for the Dominicans and an object of hostility among the Franciscans.[48] He was declared a saint on July 18, 1323, though that did not end the controversy. In 1325, Dame Prous Boneta, a Beguine (a wandering mystic religious sister), was arraigned before the Inquisition. "Speaking of her revelations, she compares Peter Olivi and Thomas Aquinas to the two brothers Abel and Cain. The original Cain had killed his brother bodily; the second Cain, recently canonized, killed his brother spiritually, which is to say, with respect to his writings. Prous Boneta had certainly not read the scholarly works of the two authors, but her deposition surely reflects the opinion of the spiritual Franciscan friars with whom she must have conversed."[49] Aquinas

---

45. Ibn Rushd, also known as *Averroes*, was a medieval Islamic philosopher who lived a century before Aquinas and wrote important commentaries on the works of Aristotle. One of his controversial ideas was that all human beings shared a single intellect. Those who shared this idea were called *Averroists*.

46. Torrell, *Saint Thomas*, 1:191–96.

47. Turner, *Thomas Aquinas*, 48.

48. Turner, *Thomas Aquinas*, 48.

49. Torrell, *Saint Thomas*, 1:322–23.

was declared a doctor of the church (a specially inspired and noteworthy theologian) in 1567 and shortly thereafter at the Council of Trent his view of the sacrament of the Eucharist as a replacement of substance, the whole substance of bread and wine being replaced by the substance of Christ's body and blood, was influential enough to guide the Council in defining the Catholic Doctrine on the matter, even if they invented a word, "transubstantiation," which Aquinas himself never used.

Over the centuries, Aquinas's importance has waxed and waned in the Catholic Church, with its heyday, perhaps, coming after Pope Leo XIII in 1879 declared that priests were to be trained primarily in theology rooted in Aquinas's own.

In our own time, there has been a reaction to that monochromatic focus on Thomism (as theology and philosophy rooted in Aquinas's thought gets called) in the Catholic Church, and many other theological approaches have been developed, but at the same time, there has been a growth in interest in Aquinas among philosophers, especially ethicists, as well as a growing awareness of the importance of Aquinas in Eastern Orthodox and Protestant circles.[50] Even when Catholic theologians reject Aquinas's view, they have very often formed their own view by reference to his.

---

50. See, for example, Plested, *Orthodox Readings*; and Svensson, *Aquinas*.

2

Tsongkhapa
A Buddhist Picture of the World

Buddhism began in India around the fifth century BC, when Siddhartha Gautama left his family and his home behind in order to find enlightenment and become free from the endless cycle of suffering. After becoming an ascetic and availing himself of all the various paths offered by the religions of his day and finding no solace, he forged his own path and achieved enlightenment sitting under a tree, earning the title "Buddha" or "enlightened one." He then gathered a community of followers and taught them his new path to others for thirty to forty-five years. Then the Buddha died and entered nirvana, leaving behind his teachings to guide future generations, so that we might also attain what he attained.

The Buddha's fundamental insights are contained in the Four Noble Truths, given by him to his associates in his first sermon after his enlightenment at the Deer Park in Sarnath.[1] The First Noble Truth is that the world is pervaded with suffering. Even those parts of life we might wish to label as satisfying are only fleeting and never fully satisfying. Thus, the world is called *samsara*, the realm of suffering. The Second Noble Truth is that our clinging attachment is the cause of suffering. Our clinging attachment also causes us to be reborn time and again, and thus we are perpetually stuck in samsara. Our clinging attachment is driven by ignorance. The elaboration of how ignorance leads to suffering which leads to ignorance in a perpetual cycle is the doctrine of the twelve-linked chain of dependent-arising. Ignorance is not the first cause of suffering. There is

---

1. For a good explanation of the Four Noble Truths, see Rahula, *What the Buddha Taught*, 16–50.

no first cause. Our suffering and our ignorance have no beginning, they have always been present in a vicious circle that perpetuates samsara. This is called *beginningless nescience*. The Third Noble Truth is that just because we have always been in samsara does not mean we cannot escape from it. The chain of dependent arising that we experience as suffering can be broken by cutting off ignorance and attachment, leading to *nirvana*, a calm beyond all conditioned formation. Nirvana is not a place or a condition. It is beyond conditioning and distinctions such as *place*. It cannot be an object of sense experience. The Fourth Noble Truth is the path to follow in cutting off samsara, which can only happen through the arising of supramundane wisdom combined with compassion that can cut the chain of dependent arising by correcting the mental errors that perpetuate it. It comprises an ethical way of life that strikes a mean between the extremes of hedonism and asceticism. Called the *Noble Eightfold Path*, it prescribes ethical norms to generate love and compassion in three areas (right speech, right action, and right livelihood); mental discipline in three areas (right effort, right attentiveness, and right concentration); and two practices to generate wisdom (right thoughts and right understanding). *Right thoughts* is minding one's thoughts so that they are about nonviolence, love for all sentient beings and detaching from samsara. *Right understanding* is about generating wisdom by understanding reality as it is.

Buddhism became widely popular throughout India and Sri Lanka, and eventually a second form developed called Mahayana ("great boat"), signifying that it was meant for saving the masses and not just the few religious adepts.[2] A tantric,[3] unbridled form of Mahayana Buddhism that utilized ecstatic visionary experiences eventually made its way to Tibet in the eighth century through the work of Padmasambhava, referred to as Guru Rinpoche ("precious teacher"). Atisha brought a second dissemination of Buddhism to Tibet in the eleventh century that was more monastic and focused on philosophy and moral living.

Tsong-kha-pa Blo-bzang-grags-pa (1357–1419) was a monastic reformer and scholastic philosopher who worked to integrate these two streams of Buddhism in Tibet by providing a systematic vision that could

---

2. Tsongkhapa often refers to *Hinayana* (small boat) Buddhism, by which he means all forms of Buddhism other than Mahayana, which typically stress individual attainment over communal salvation.

3. *Tantric* refers to forms of Buddhism that utilize secret mantras, specific body positioning, symbolic mandala images, and visualization of dieties to make religious practices more powerful and effective.

hold them together, acknowledging the power of tantric practices but recommending a slower, methodical, philosophical, and meditative path for most people to guard against the corrupting dangers of unbridled tantric practices.[4] His powerful new synthesis and disciplined way of life revitalized monastic life in Tibet. While his teachings sought to integrate ideas from all of the major schools of Buddhist thought in Tibet, Tsongkhapa gathered some like-minded disciples and built the Ganden monastery in 1409 where his own views were taught. His followers built two more monasteries during his lifetime, Drepung in 1416 and Sera in 1419, and thus was born a new school of thought based on the teachings of Tsongkhapa. Called *Gelukpa* (the "virtuous ones"), today it is the largest and most influential group within Tibetan Buddhism and its leader, the Dalai Lama, is the *de facto* spiritual leader of the Tibetan people.

Our Situation

You and I are humans, which is relatively fortunate, since there are much worse things to be. You and I also have the ability and leisure to read and to think, as indicated by your having time to read this book, so again, we are living fortunate lives. We experience a world in which people are born and die, have joys and sorrows, triumphs and failures, and struggle to live and find the meaning of it all. We seek happiness, and only find it in a limited way, mixed with sorrows and suffering. This is the First Noble Truth. The experience of living a human life is good and bad. But there is a deeper reality, nirvana, in which there are no struggles, no failures nor triumphs, and no death nor birth. The world of our experience so overwhelms us that we cannot see the deeper reality through the flood of data from our senses, the veil of our emotions, and the chatter of our thinking. So different is this ultimate reality that it cannot even be described with the words we learn from this work-a-day world.

The world of our experience, however, can be described in words and it follows definite laws. The good things that happen to us, and the bad, are the result of actions we have taken in previous lives, resulting in consequences that we experience once the seeds we have planted come to fruition.[5] This is *karma*. The laws of karma describe how certain causes

---

4. Jinpa, *Self*. For more on Tsongkhapa's life see Berzin, "Life of Tsongkhapa," or Samuel, *Civilized Shamans*, 429–524.

5. Tsongkhapa, *Great Treatise*, 1:209–14.

necessarily lead to certain effects in future lifetimes when the conditions finally ripen. We are reborn in this realm of mundane experience because of the laws of karma and our attachment to experiences and ultimately to our sense of self. We seek peace and never really find it. Our misguided efforts just get us further enmeshed in this cycle of rebirth.

These forced rebirths are like a bad dream from which we cannot seem to awaken. This world of experience is not ultimately real, but it seems real to us. We have no way of knowing for how long this dream has been going on, but there is a way to wake up, discovered by Siddhartha Gautama, the Buddha, and perfected in Tibet.

We do not have to accept any of this on faith. "There is a systematic training that can lead to the empirical conclusion that a continuity of consciousness transcends the limitations of one body, one life."[6] This training predates Buddhism, but it has been perfected in Tibet. Through it one can calm the mind enough to experience one's own previous lives in ways that can be objectively corroborated.

A Picture

Tibetan Buddhist monasteries have many images, statues, symbols, and paintings to help people internalize Buddhist teachings, which are beyond any image or explanation. One painting, the *Wheel of Life*, shown in figure 2.1, depicts the entire process of rebirth, its causes, and the six realms into which one might be reborn. It appears next to the doorway in most Tibetan temples, and its outline is said to have been designed by the Buddha himself.[7]

---

6. The Dalai Lama, quoted in Luisi, *Mind and Life*, 163.

7. For a longer description of the spiritual significance of the *Wheel of Life*, see Jeffrey Hopkin's introduction in Gyatso, *Meaning of Life*, 1–28.

PICTURES OF THE WORLD

Figure 2.1: The *Wheel of Life*, as depicted on a sacred thangka painting. It depicts the six realms into which one might be reborn, as well as the major factors that drive rebirth.

The *Wheel of Life* depicts a disk of four concentric circles being held by a fierce monster. The disk represents the world as we experience it—samsara, cyclical existence, the endless cycle of rebirths in which we are trapped. The monster represents impermanence, which keeps the wheel spinning. Often the monster is depicted as Yama, the king of hell and lord of death, underscoring and personalizing what is meant by impermanence. At the top right, the Buddha stands outside the wheel showing that he is beyond the vicissitudes of cyclic existence. He holds one hand out indicating that he is teaching, and the other hand points to liberation, depicted sometimes as the moon, but here as a pure land of enlightenment in the upper left. The Buddha exists outside our world of experience, and the promise of Buddhism is that we can also escape from the wheel of life and achieve the freedom of enlightenment.

There are two fundamentally different levels of truth on display here—there is what is immediately apparent about the world, called *conventional truth*, and what is ultimately true about it, *ultimate truth*.[8] We will have much to say about the wheel of life—samsara—but what is ultimately true is that there is nothing fixed about it. It has no ultimate existence. On a conventional level, we experience a world of joy and suffering that was here long before we were born and that will be here long after we have died. We believe that most of what happens in this conventional world of experience is beyond our control. But the deeper truth is that this entire world of cyclic existence is ultimately an illusion of our own making. It is a powerful illusion, and we have to work to see through it, but seeing through it is possible and is called *enlightenment*.

Figure 2.2: In the center of the *Wheel of Life*, a pig, a rooster, and a snake symbolize the three poisons of ignorance, hatred, and desire.

8. More about the two truths can be found at Tsongkhapa, *Great Treatise*, 3:218.

Turning again to the painting, figure 2.2 shows the center of the wheel where three figures—a pig, a rooster, and a snake—mutually create themselves, each issuing from another's mouth in a circle. They represent the fundamental poisons on which the wheel turns: ignorance, hatred, and desire. The pig represents ignorance, as pigs sleep in the dirtiest places and eat whatever is in front of them. The snake represents hostility or hatred, as snakes strike with the smallest provocation. The rooster pictured is an Asian bird that has an inordinate attachment to its mate, and so represents desire or attachment. The fundamental poison is ignorance, because if we are not reflective, we believe that things exist ultimately as we experience them—we mistakenly equate conventional truth with ultimate truth.[9] We experience some things as good or evil, helpful or dangerous, pleasurable or painful, and unreflectively think that they have these characteristics intrinsically, by their very nature, and that this is their ultimate essence, what is ultimately true about them. But this is never the case. Nothing in the wheel of life is fixed. All things change and have no ultimate fixed essence. If we experience some things as good, helpful, or pleasurable we become attached to them. If we experience other things as evil, dangerous, or painful we become hostile toward them. Either way, we unreflectively superimpose either attractiveness or unattractiveness on their allegedly intrinsic nature and then behave accordingly, leading to greater ignorance by further obscuring the fact that ultimately they have no intrinsic nature at all. They are neither essentially good nor essentially evil. It is this enslaving collaboration between experience and ignorance that keeps us trapped in cyclical rebirth, spinning around the wheel of life. While the explanation of this process began with ignorance, this does not mean that rebirth had a beginning. From beginningless time these three poisons have worked together.[10]

Around the three poisons in the *Wheel of Life* is a black and white ring with figures moving up and down around the wheel. Against a black background figures are being bound by their actions and dragged down toward the lower realms. On the other side, against a white background, people are moving to the higher realms due to virtuous actions. For the unenlightened,

---

9. For a description of how the three poisons trap us in samsara see Tsongkhapa, *Great Treatise*, 3:183.

10. "Buddhism . . . accepts the beginningless continuum of consciousness, therefore it also accepts the beginningless continuum of sentient beings. Because sentient beings have no beginning, Buddhism interprets the evolution of the physical universe as intimately interdependent with the sentient beings who inhabit and experience the external world" (The Dalai Lama in Luisi, *Mind and Life*, 183).

rebirth is not a matter of choice. Rebirth is determined by our past actions governed by the laws of karma. There are two categories of actions: virtuous and non-virtuous.[11] Virtuous actions, such as studying dharma[12] and living ethically, cause us to be reborn in higher realms and bring us positive experiences in any realm. Non-virtuous actions, such as stealing and killing, cause us to be reborn in lower realms and bring about negative experiences in any realm. No one enforces the laws of karma. They simply describe the way that cyclical existence works. The laws of karma only apply to beings enmeshed in samsara, like me and, I presume, like you. Enlightened beings such as the Buddha transcend the laws of karma and are not affected by them. Buddhas can choose to be reborn in a particular place or can choose not to be reborn at all. We will say more about this later.

The third circle from the center on the *Wheel of Life* depicts the six realms into which we might be reborn. There are three upper realms of relative peace, plentitude, and happiness, and three lower realms of relative diminishment, suffering, and unhappiness.

Figure 2.3: Detail from the *Wheel of Life* showing part of the hell realm where beings are tortured by hideous beasts and flames. The curve at the bottom holds two of the panels of the twelve-linked chain of dependent-arising: Contact, symbolized by a man and a woman sleeping together, and Experience, symbolized by being shot in the eye with an arrow.

To give a sense, figure 2.3 shows part of the depiction of the hell realm, with people being tortured in various ways by hideous beasts. The upper realms

---

11. For an explanation of how karma works see Tsongkhapa, *Great Treatise*, 209–46.

12. *Dharma* is the word most often used by Tibetan Buddhists to talk about the teachings of the Buddha and the fundamental laws that govern reality.

are our human realm, a semi-divine realm and a divine realm. The divine realm is one of maximal peace and joy, but it is still a realm of cyclical existence. A rebirth in the divine realm will be happy, but it will eventually come to an end because it is still subject to the twelve-linked chain of dependent-arising. The happiness and peace in this realm are therefore not ultimate.[13] The human realm represents the most fortunate rebirth, because humans have the ability to hear and understand the teachings of the Buddha and humans struggle enough to be motivated to put them into practice in order to get off the wheel of life, becoming enlightened buddhas in their own right.[14] The three lower realms of diminishment are the animal realm, the hungry ghost realm and the hell realm. Animals can hear the teachings of Buddha, but they cannot understand them, and their lives are a struggle. The hell realm is full of suffering and torture, and beings there are so distracted that they give no thought to the teachings of the Buddha, which could end their suffering. But hell is not forever. The bad karma that caused a rebirth in a hell realm will eventually wear itself out and then one will be reborn in a higher realm. The Buddha appears in each of the realms. Being enlightened and free from the constraints of karma governing cyclical existence, the Buddha is able to appear and offer teaching in each of the six realms without getting enmeshed in any of them.

The outermost circle of the wheel depicts the twelve specific steps by which we are trapped in the cycle of rebirth because of our ignorance and emotions, the twelve-linked chain of dependent-arising. This is an important yet difficult idea at the center of Buddhist philosophy, to which we now turn.

---

13. There are other forms of Buddhism in which being reborn in a divine realm is the ultimate goal. The most famous of these is Pure Land Buddhism, which holds that the buddha Amitabha, through his own merit, has created the Pure Land of Sukhavati, a buddha field of great bliss and pure teachings. One can be reborn in Sukhavati through having recourse to Amitabha and remain in it forever, or achieve enlightenment directly from there. Tsongkhapa does not subscribe to these teachings. For more, see Williams, *Mahayana Buddhism*, 238–54.

14. To be able to progress well, one also needs to be born in a place that is not in a state of war, where Buddhist teachings are available, and into a life-situation that allows for formal education and leisure to study, which is a very rare situation. For a further explanation, see Tsongkhapa, *Great Treatise*, 1:117–76.

Emptiness and the Human Person

Dependent-arising refers to the simultaneous creation of multiple things, each in dependence upon the other. For example, the titles *mother* and *daughter* arise dependently upon the birth of a girl. This one is called *daughter* because she came from her mother. That one is called *mother* because she gave birth to a daughter. Left and right, and before and after, are other examples of terms that obviously arise dependently.

An important insight into the world is that everything in it arises dependently. Everything comes to be due to causes and conditions, and therefore arises dependently with these causes and conditions. Nothing comes to be without causes. Nothing creates itself. If something had an intrinsic nature, it would exist without causes and conditions, but this is impossible.[15] Thus, we say that all things are empty of intrinsic existence. To understand, we use the example of a chariot.[16] We all know chariots exist. We can talk about them and we could ride in one, but in what way does a chariot exist? Here we are not investigating the *idea* of a chariot, for that exists in a different way than the real chariot does. We are investigating the existence of a real chariot. A chariot exists in dependence upon its parts: the wheels, carriage, tongue, etc. If these do not exist, the chariot cannot exist. Even if these parts exist, they have to be assembled in a particular way for there to be a chariot, so the chariot is also something more than its parts. The chariot functions when these parts are assembled and thus exists at the conventional level, but it does not have an *essence* hiding underneath the parts as some additional part. The chariot exists in dependence on its parts, not apart from them, and it is more than the sum of its parts, but not in a way that transcends the parts or can leave them behind. Thus, we say that the chariot has conventional or dependent existence and it is ultimately empty of absolute existence.

This emptiness is a fundamental point of Buddhist philosophy. It does not mean that things do not exist at all. Things exist dependently upon other things, causes, and conditions. Ultimately, however, nothing exists intrinsically, in a fixed way or by its own nature. Even the Buddha only exists conventionally and has no intrinsic nature or ultimate existence.[17] Things are affected by other things and they change. Nothing remains un-

---

15. Tsongkhapa, *Great Treatise*, 3:137.
16. Tsongkhapa, *Great Treatise*, 3:283.
17. Tsongkhapa, *Great Treatise*, 3:218.

changing. This is how all things function. It is particularly important to affirm that what is true for all things is also true about the human person. People have conventional existence. People do not have ultimate existence or an intrinsic nature.[18] People are not unchanging. People do not exist in their own right. People come to be due to causes and conditions, and they constantly change as they encounter other causes and conditions.

People are made up of five parts or aggregates, called *skandhas*: 1) a material body and its energies, 2) with a stream of sensations, 3) that get processed into a stream of thoughts and judgments, 4) under the influence of particular habits and conditioning, 5) and a conscious awareness.[19] Each of these skandhas is constantly changing, but together they give rise to the appearance that there is something more, something solid behind them, something that holds them together and in which they are embedded. This extra thing some would call a *soul* or a *self*, but it does not exist. There is only the appearance of a soul.

The appearance of a soul is analogous to the illusions created by Moiré patterns which occur when one regular pattern is superimposed on another regular pattern, creating fringes of interference. The interference can appear to us as a third pattern, distinct from the two original patterns.

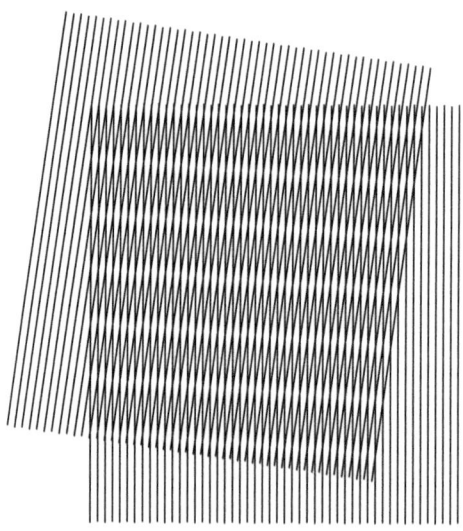

Figure 2.4: Example of a Moiré pattern with two sets of parallel lines. Where they overlap, they give the appearance of horizontal bands.

18. Tsongkhapa, *Great Treatise*, 3:215.
19. Gyatso, *Meaning of Life*, 54–55.

For example, see figure 2.4. When a series of vertical lines is superimposed on an identical set of lines that has been slightly rotated, dark and light horizontal bands appear. In reality, there are only the two sets of nearly vertical lines, there are no horizontal bands. But there is also undoubtedly the appearance of horizontal bands. In the same way, a person is composed of only the five skandhas, but when these five skandhas are seen superimposed on one another, there is the appearance of soul.

This is an example of the way that ignorance leads us astray. We experience ourselves and others in flux and mistakenly posit that there is something fixed about us. We can use the word "self" because the self exists conventionally. "Self" refers to the object of a conscious awareness that thinks "I."[20] Our self exists in dependence upon our aggregates giving rise to our awareness, but our self has no intrinsic existence apart from these. So the self has no ultimate existence, only dependent existence. The soul, however, is mere appearance and does not exist even conventionally. Buddhism thus asserts no-soul ("*anatman*").

There is no soul reincarnated in rebirth, losing one body and getting a new one. Rather, because of the twelve-linked chain of dependent-arising, the conventionally existing self causes a new birth to come about at its dissolution. Like the image of a signet ring in a wax seal, where there is nothing of the ring in the seal except its image, the new skandhas called together bear the marks of the old skandhas that are dispersing. But the causality is more complex than simply one life leading into the next. Assuming that you are in a human rebirth as you read this, there had to be a cause in a former life for this human rebirth. The cause must have been relatively good, since being born into the human realm is a fortunate rebirth, but the primary cause of any particular rebirth does not have to be an action in the life that immediately preceded this one. The seeds planted by actions in any life can possibly take thousands of lifetimes to ripen into a new rebirth. Karmic consequences are never lost, though they can be delayed for millions of lifetimes. Also, there are many particular conditions about your current rebirth into the human realm. Each of these particulars might have been the fruition of karmic seeds laid down in different lifetimes. No single line connects your past life to this life. Instead, there is a web of connections between this current life and past karmic actions, and we are all spinning a complex web of karmic causality through the myriad

20. Tsongkhapa, *Great Treatise*, 3:215.

actions we take in this life that connects us to the many future lives we might live in any of the six realms.

Specifically, the twelve-linked chain of dependent-arising asserts is that 1) ignorance in some former life led to 2) actions that were performed that had a 3) karmic causality on our mind-stream, leaving some mark that has remained over one or many lifetimes. This cause finally ripened, creating 4) a new embryonic human person, us, that has developed 5) senses that bring us 6) into contact with the world. Once we begin 7) experiencing the world we 8) become attached to what we experience as good and adverse to what we experience as bad. This was described above in the section on the three poisons. We then 9) try to hold on to the things to which we are attached and push away the things we dislike. These actions have immediate effects in our life, but also have long-term karmic consequences. At the end of our life, we have 10) accumulated enough karmic potency to give rise to another lifetime. This will result in 11) a future rebirth that will have its day and eventually lead to 12) another death.[21]

The twelve links are a central example of dependent-arising. No step forward in the chain has absolute existence. Each one arises because of previous causes and conditions that have come to fruition. Together, they cause the bad karma and afflictions that generate our rebirth time and again in samsara. The best place to break this cycle is to sever the affliction of attachment that defines link eight so that experiencing does not lead to grasping.[22] If the chain of causation is broken here by having no affliction, then, even if we have accumulated much bad karma, there will be no rebirth. Much of Buddhist practice is therefore aimed at uncovering this truth and helping people let go of attachment. Let us therefore turn to these two topics: what actions are helpful and harmful and how do we know what we know?

Ethics

The inexorable laws of karma provide the starting point for ethics. Since all actions have karmic consequences tied to future rebirths, it behooves us to perform virtuous actions that lead to better rebirths rather than

---

21. For a good explanation of the twelve-linked chain of dependent-arising, see Gyatso, *Meaning of Life*, 3–27, 38–51, 57–62.

22. For more on why it is best to break this specific link, see the comments on affliction in Tsongkhapa, *Great Treatise*, 1:59, 298, 335.

non-virtuous actions that lead to lower ones.[23] Ethics is not a matter of what one "should" do based on abstract principles, but a knowledge of the laws of karma that gives one control over future rebirths by understanding the specific causes and conditions that give rise to particular states of rebirth and acting accordingly. In Mahayana Buddhism there is also the bodhisattva ideal to keep in mind: that one's actions should be dedicated to end the suffering of all sentient beings and not just to achieve a better rebirth for one's own mind-stream. "The Bodhisattva's compassion aids wisdom's undercutting of self-centeredness, and his or her developing wisdom ensures that compassionate action is appropriate, effective, and not covertly self-seeking."[24] The foundation of virtue is attaining certain knowledge of karma and its effects.[25] There is no divine creator or primal essence that causes happiness or suffering.[26] Pleasant and unpleasant situations are caused by virtuous and non-virtuous karma tied to specific actions in past lives. In order to be protected from painful rebirths, we need to refrain from non-virtuous actions that cause painful rebirths in future lives. In order to generate happiness in future rebirths, we need to perform actions that cause happiness in future rebirths.

Karmic causality is never wasted. Seeds laid down in one life will surely have effects in future lives when they come to fruition. But the connections between actions and effects are quite complex and rely on a number of factors. For instance, killing is a non-virtuous action with terrible karmic consequences. The karmic ramifications are the same if you perform the action yourself or hire someone to kill for you, but they are different if you accidentally kill the wrong person instead, and you would avoid the consequences altogether if you died before the actual killing took place since you would have assumed another life at that point. The killing would become weightier if you delighted in it or tortured your victim, but would have less effect if you felt ashamed or contrite. It would be more serious if your victim were poor or pleading for mercy, or someone close to you, or a more excellent being such as a guru or bodhisattva. It would also be worse if you were doing it based on a wrong view, such as a religiously motivated animal sacrifice. There are

23. For Tsongkhapa's view of ethics based on the laws of karma, see Tsongkhapa, *Great Treatise*, 1:209–46, which forms the basis for this section. For a longer treatment of Mahayana Buddhist ethics not specific to Tsongkhapa see Harvey, *Introduction*, chap. 3, "Mahayana Emphasis and adaptations."

24. Harvey, *Introduction*, 125.

25. Tsongkhapa, *Great Treatise*, 3:211.

26. Tsongkhapa, *Great Treatise*, 3:210.

instances, however, when killing could also be virtuous. For instance, if a bodhisattva saw a robber who was about to kill hundreds of monks for the sake of material gain—an action that would surely cause the robber to go straight to hell for many lifetimes of torment—and out of compassion killed the robber instead, risking a single rebirth in hell while saving the robber from a far worse fate, there would be no fault.[27] Such an action would be meritorious since the net karmic effect would be positive.

There are also standard religious practices one could perform in order to ameliorate the effects of negative karma. One could seek refuge in the three jewels: the Buddha, the dharma, and the sangha. The Buddha is the one who teaches refuge. The sangha is the community of those who follow the Buddha and thus assist in accomplishing refuge. The dharma is the sum total of the teachings of Buddhism, and it is the real refuge since it is the teaching once learned that liberates one from fear.[28] Even for beginners, seeking refuge in the three jewels begins to eliminate faults and bring about knowledge that builds good qualities. There are also common practices to live out and strengthen one's commitment to the dharma such as prayer, having a shrine in one's home with images of the Buddha and venerable teachers, lighting butter candles in dedicated places, and circumambulating stupas (circular piles of stone built over a holy relic, serving as a monument to a buddha's enlightenment). These practices are commonly undertaken by lay practitioners and have many beneficial effects.

One can also intensify the karmic consequences of one's actions, for good and for ill, by undertaking vows, placing one on a different level of practice and holding one to a different level of ethics. One can reach the first level of excellence while remaining a lay practitioner or *householder* by simply embracing Buddhist teachings and vowing to refrain from non-virtuous actions such as killing, lying, stealing, unchastity, and becoming intoxicated. Beyond this, monks[29] make a vow to live more strict lives of dedication to the dharma, vowing to fast and to refrain from dancing, wearing makeup or perfume, sleeping in soft beds, and accumulating wealth. On the highest level, one can vow to pursue one's practice for the sake of all suffering sentient beings, thus becoming a bodhisattva. Bodhisattvas take

---

27. Harvey, *Introduction*, 136–37.

28. Tsongkhapa, *Great Treatise*, 1:207.

29. *Bhiksu* in Sanskrit, and often referred to as *shravakas* or *solitary realizers* in the Mahayana tradition, since they work to achieve their own, solitary enlightenment. For delineation of the three types of persons see Tsongkhapa, *Great Treatise*, 1:131.

on the practices of Mahayana Buddhism, which further specifies and intensifies the effects of their practice. It is said hyperbolically that a bodhisattva simply holding a lamp wick in front of a stupa obtains more merit than if all the inhabitants of three billion world systems each were to offer a candle the size of a mountain.[30]

More importantly, with knowledge and the assistance of a master, it is possible to forge a better karmic destiny, attenuating the bad karma and amplifying good karma that has been created in former lives. When done properly, combinations of practices such as confessing sins, reciting mantras, making icons of the Buddha, worshipping images or stupas, turning away from non-virtuous actions and taking refuge in the three jewels can be quite effective. It can weaken the capacity of negative karma to bear fruit, shortening the duration or intensity of suffering, or even changing karma that would have caused a rebirth in a miserable realm to instead merely cause a temporary headache in a better realm. Positive karmic threads can be amplified through further directed positive actions, but they can also be amplified by tapping into a reserve of karmic fruits amassed by a great teacher.[31]

Mahayana Buddhism shifts the goals of Theravadan Buddhism. Instead of personally seeking to escape the suffering cycle of samsara, Mahayana Buddhism promotes the goal of *bodhicitta* or *the spirit of enlightenment*, which is to end the suffering of all sentient beings.[32] Instead of entering nirvana, a state of peace, one seeks to become a buddha oneself and enter the state of *nonabiding nirvana*, still engaged with the world of samsara because of compassion but, by achieving great wisdom, no longer controlled by it so that you can work effectively for others.[33] "You need wisdom to prevent falling into the extreme of cyclic existence, and you need compassion to prevent falling into the extreme of peace [nirvana], so wisdom does not prevent you from falling into the extreme of peace."[34]

Bodhicitta offers a higher goal, beyond ordinary ethics, where one dedicates all of one's practice toward the benefit of all sentient beings. Those who seek this are called *bodhisattvas*. The highest stages of the Buddhist

---

30. Tsongkhapa, *Great Treatise*, 1:234.
31. Tsongkhapa, *Great Treatise*, 1:214.
32. Tsongkhapa, *Great Treatise*, 1:18.
33. Tsongkhapa, *Great Treatise*, 1:46.
34. Tsongkhapa, *Great Treatise*, 2:19.

path thus call for practices that generate both wisdom and compassion[35] to empower bodhisattvas with the abilities they need to lead others out of suffering and into enlightenment by generating the six perfections: generosity, ethical discipline, patience, joyous perseverance, meditative stabilization, and the perfection of wisdom.[36] Generosity is an attitude of nonattachment toward possessions generated by intentionally giving them away.[37] To be effective, generosity should be practiced evenly toward friends and foes alike without waiting for others to ask or expecting anything in return, even praise.[38] In order to help others, bodhisattvas need ethical discipline: to practice restraint, accumulate virtue, and steadfastly act for the welfare of other living beings. This is done by holding oneself to strict standards and as one progresses, it gets easier and generates many other benefits such as eliminating the seeds of wrongdoing and garnering respect from others.[39] "Patience is (1) disregarding harm done to you, (2) accepting the suffering arising in your mind-stream, and (3) being certain about the teachings and firmly maintaining belief in them."[40] We can practice patience by recognizing that those who harm us are doing so out of ignorance and so are suffering themselves. Thus, instead of being angry with them or wishing them harm, we will seek to help them.[41] Joyous perseverance or delighting in virtue is found by reflecting on the benefits of following the bodhisattva path and recognizing that we can do it wherever we are.[42] It is important to stop any form of discouragement, laziness, or self-contempt, lest it be like the tip of a poisoned arrow piercing our armor, eventually killing us through the smallest cut.[43]

The final two perfections, meditative stabilization and the perfection of wisdom, are the most difficult. They are attained by combining specific forms of one-pointed meditation focused on our own minds with philosophical analysis that seeks to understand the meditation and the true nature of the self. As we go back and forth between these two activities, we get

---

35. Tsongkhapa, *Great Treatise*, 2:21.
36. Tsongkhapa, *Great Treatise*, 2:86–91.
37. Tsongkhapa, *Great Treatise*, 2:114–15.
38. Tsongkhapa, *Great Treatise*, 2:124–26.
39. Tsongkhapa, *Great Treatise*, 2:144–47.
40. Tsongkhapa, *Great Treatise*, 2:152.
41. Tsongkhapa, *Great Treatise*, 2:159–61.
42. Tsongkhapa, *Great Treatise*, 2:182–92.
43. Tsongkhapa, *Great Treatise*, 2:186–207.

a clearer understanding of the self, leading to a more focused meditation, yielding higher and higher clarity. To understand the process, let us step back and examine truth itself and how we can know it.

Truth and Knowledge

There are two levels of truth, what is conventionally true about the world and what is ultimately true about it, particularly its status in being.[44] Conventional truth appears to our senses. Buddhism counts six senses, the five counted in the West and the mind, which is aware of our thoughts. These are also called "consciousnesses," as in "our visual consciousness." There are three simple criteria for conventional truth: 1) it is known through sense data, 2) it is not contradicted by other sense data, and 3) it is not contradicted by reason.[45] The first principle simply means that we are to rely on our senses as primary sources of information about the world. The second principle distinguishes between normal impressions and dreams, delusions, and mistakes, as when we see a rope on the ground and think it is a snake. Upon further inspection we see the mistake, just as we recognize that we were dreaming once we awaken. Rather than appealing to a philosophical system, we use simple reason to determine what is true when our sense data seems to be contradictory.

The third principle, determining if something is contrary to reason, requires greater effort. Our senses do not simply report about the world, they elaborate upon it, reifying it, adding the idea that the objects perceived intrinsically exist in the way that we perceive them. This is called *maya* ("*avidyā*" in Sanskrit), and it is a fundamental truth about the world. For instance, we see with our visual consciousness. Our visual consciousness is more than just the eye, it includes the way the mind makes sense of the data coming from the eye.[46] The visual consciousness can identify the color and shape of an object. But what the visual consciousness actually reports is the color and shape of the object and the idea that this object

---

44. For a short synopsis of the relation of ultimate and conventional truth in the Gelukpa system see Magee, *Nature of Things*, 23–24.

45. Tsongkhapa, *Great Treatise*, 3:178–79.

46. Modern science shows that the data coming from the retina is already processed for edge and object detection, and objects are tagged for motion and position in space before data gets handed on to the brain. This kind of preprocessing is some of what the Buddhists mean by speaking of the visual consciousness rather than simply speaking of the eye.

actually exists. The visual consciousness cannot determine if something actually exists, but reports it nonetheless. Existence is the proper object of the mind, the reasoning consciousness. To uncritically accept the report of the visual consciousness that *existence* is true about the object would be the same as to accept as fact that someone was making sound simply because we saw her lips moving. Sight does not give us information about sound, nor can it tell us about existence. In the same way, the reasoning consciousness cannot tell us if something is appearing to the visual consciousness. Only the visual consciousness can tell us that. The reasoning consciousness tells us if the appearance is true, if something actually exists in the way that it is appearing.[47]

The object of reasoning consciousness is never a conventional object per se, for instance the person standing in front of me. The object of reasoning consciousness in this case would be the *essential existence* of the person standing in front of me—does this person have an intrinsic essence or eternal soul? We see that there is a person standing in front of us. Visual consciousness establishes their form. But we cannot see if this person has intrinsic existence. We have to use our reason to establish that.[48] We can see their color and shape with our visual consciousness, we can hear them with our sound consciousness, and these consciousnesses also assure us that the person exists intrinsically.[49] But they cannot do the last part. They are deceiving us about this.

Only our reasoning consciousness can establish if the person exists intrinsically, and it can only do this through both analyzing the current data from the other consciousnesses and performing a philosophical analysis of the final status of being. The philosophical analysis reveals that emptiness is the real nature of all things, so this person cannot have an intrinsic existence.[50] Emptiness means that all things, like the chariot and the person standing in front of me, are empty of intrinsic existence.[51] As with the other senses, the reasoning consciousness could be mistaken due to impairment or error. Impairment requires correction and this is not always possible. Errors

---

47. Tsongkhapa, *Great Treatise*, 3:156. It is also noted as Chandrakirti's position: "What [Chandrakirti] refutes is that visual consciousnesses and such are valid with regard to a special object-reality—and not that they are valid with regard to other objects" (Tsongkhapa, *Great Treatise*, 3:164).

48. Tsongkhapa, *Great Treatise*, 3:165.

49. Tsongkhapa, *Great Treatise*, 3:182.

50. Tsongkhapa, *Great Treatise*, 3:156.

51. Tsongkhapa, *Great Treatise*, 3:111.

can be corrected through further analysis, so the mind must be trained and focused on this task. But when the mind has been trained and is free of error, it correctly establishes that all things are empty of intrinsic existence.

Once we become absolutely sure of the nonexistence of the intrinsic nature that appears, we no longer grasp objects. We have broken the twelve-linked chain of dependent-arising and conquered our affliction. We will not have to be reborn. This is the ultimate goal of some Buddhist systems. Mind-streams that have this realization will not have to be reborn in samsara. When they die, their suffering is quenched and they can enter a nirvana of peace. But this is not enough for the bodhisattva. "Bodhisattvas, not content with mere liberation from cyclic existence through the mere extinction of afflictions, seek buddhahood for the sake of all living beings; hence they meditate so as to utterly extinguish cognitive obscurations. Thus, they meditate for a very long time and are adorned with limitless collections of merit and wisdom."[52] For buddhas, who see the world just as it is, there is not even the appearance of a self coming from the visual consciousness nor generated in meditation. Such appearances would hamper their ability to function omnisciently on behalf of all sentient beings, even though they would not cause affliction. Those who ceased meditating when they had merely overcome afflicting errors would still have erroneous appearances. "Certain latent propensities are firmly set in the mind-stream through its being beginninglessly suffused with strong attachment to things regarded as intrinsically existent; these latent propensities give rise to errors of dualistic appearance, so that things appear to be intrinsically existent when they are not."[53] It is the compassion for the suffering of others that keeps bodhisattvas meditating and working on the other perfections after they have removed their own afflictions. Thus, it is that we can only achieve the goal of bodhicitta, becoming buddhas in our own right to help all sentient beings, through wisdom combined with compassion.

To summarize the final stage of the path to enlightenment, one can finally and completely see through the deluded view of *self* that binds us by alternating back and forth between insight meditation and philosophical analysis, each deepening the other:

> When you have found the view of what has definitive meaning, you will have determined that the self and that which belongs to the self do not intrinsically exist in the basis in relation to which the

---

52. Tsongkhapa, *Great Treatise*, 3:322.
53. Tsongkhapa, *Great Treatise*, 3:323.

conceptions of "I" and "mine" arise. And just as when you initially made this determination, you continue to use extensive analysis with discriminating wisdom to bring the force of certainty to bear upon that conclusion. You alternate between stabilizing meditation—which stays with that conclusion without scattering—and analysis with discriminating wisdom. At that time, if stability decreases due to excessive analytical meditation, do more stabilizing meditation and restore stability. As stability increases under the influence of extensive stabilizing meditation, if you lose interest in analysis and thus fail to analyze, then your ascertainment of reality will not become firm and powerful. In the absence of a firm and powerful ascertainment of reality, you will not do even the slightest damage to the countervailing superimpositions which conceive of the existence of the two selves. Therefore, cultivate a balance of serenity and insight by doing extensive analytical meditation.[54]

Tsongkhapa and the Tibetan Buddhist Tradition

As many others had done and would continue to do, Tsongkhapa forged a new synthesis of shamanic and clerical traditions that had been woven into Tibetan Buddhism. For many reasons, however, some historical and others philosophical, Tsongkhapa's opinions have endured within Tibetan Buddhism to a much larger degree than any other single Tibetan scholar.[55] It has been argued as to whether or not he intended to found a new religious order within Tibetan Buddhism or to simply reform and reinvigorate the existing monastic structure, but his followers certainly took the path of separation for the sake of maintaining Tsongkhapa's vision in its purity. Their Gelukpa order still uses his teachings and the other works he sanctioned as their primary curriculum.

At first, the Gelukpa order was simply one among many sub-traditions within Tibetan Buddhism, some being more clerical, some more shamanic, some monastic, and others yogic. The Gelukpas were led by the Dalai Lama, the recognized reincarnation of one of Tsongkhapa's younger disciples, Gendun Drub (1391–1474), who was also recognized as an emanation of Avalokiteshvara, the Buddha of Compassion. In around 1578, the third leader of the Gelukpas converted the Mongol leader Altan Khan to

---

54. Tsongkhapa, *Great Treatise*, 3:351–52.
55. The historical development in this section follows Samuel, *Civilized Shamans*, 525–52.

Buddhism and received the title "Dalai" meaning "ocean" for the depths of his teaching, thus beginning an alliance between the Gelukpa order and the Mongols. The fourth Dalai Lama was born in the family of the Altan Khan's grandson. The fifth Dalai Lama (1617–82) finally prevailed over the other Tibetan spiritual leader to make friends with the Mongols, the Karmapa, and was proclaimed the temporal and spiritual leader of Tibet, while his Mongol ally, Gushri Khan, was named King of Tibet. This arrangement allowed the Gelukpas to leverage temporal power to spread their religious views and they became the largest, most important order within Tibet. The fifth Dalai Lama was not a religious purist and was not hostile to other sub-traditions, but he built up the network of Gelukpa monasteries and eventually shut down the rival Jonangpa order, forcibly converting its monasteries into Gelukpa institutions.

In the eighteenth century, Jigmed Lingpa (1730–98) created a new synthesis of Tibetan Buddhism through a combination of ideas from two non-Gelukpa lineages, Nyingma and Dzogchen. His synthesis proved immensely influential, giving rise to a non-sectarian movement that continues to this day as the main rival to Gelukpa thought, Rimed (pronounced ree-may). Rimed scholars consciously embrace all forms of Tibetan Buddhism and even embrace elements of Bon, a Tibetan religion that predates the introduction of Buddhism into Tibet. At the time, the Gelukpas had become stale and arid, with most Geluk scholars simply writing commentaries on Tsongkhapa's and his early followers' texts that hewed closely to the originals. In contrast, Rimed scholars were renewing and reenergizing their traditions with original thought through renewed study of older Indian texts and lively meditation practices.

In the twentieth century the thirteenth Dalai Lama (1876–1933) worked to transform Tibet into an effective centralized state and to modernize the Gelukpa monastic system. While he was open to embracing other traditions, his second in command within the Gelukpas was narrowly sectarian and worked to reestablish Gelukpa hegemonies. The political reforms the thirteenth Dalai Lama put in place were not strong enough to endure after his death, and the Tibetan government was not able to resist the Chinese when their communist regime decided to integrate Tibet into its territory in 1950. After a failed uprising, the Fourteenth Dalai Lama (b. 1935) was forced to flee in 1959 and now lives in Dharamsala, India. He is the *de facto* spiritual leader of Tibet, and as such believes that he should protect all varieties of Tibetan Buddhism, not simply his own Geluk tradition, though he ultimately sides with his own tradition when asked questions about Buddhism.[56] Given that the Gelukpa tradition is still rooted in the writings of Tsongkhapa, we could say that, currently, in religious authority within Tibetan Buddhism, Tsongkhapa is first among equals.

56. One of the authors was able to ask the Dalai Lama a direct question about a controversial area that divides Tibetan Buddhism—the ultimate status of the tathagatagarbha. Tsongkhapa was adamantly on one side of this issue. The Dalai Lama was surprisingly open to affirming the truth and insight of the rival position, against Tsongkhapa's view. When asked to clarify if he was really affirming the contrary position, the Dalai Lama said the rival position was true on the conventional level, but Tsongkhapa's view was true on the ultimate level.

3

Steven Pinker
A Naturalist Picture of the World

Steven Pinker (b. 1954) is a modern experimental psychologist working at Harvard University who explores the mind, language development, and human nature. Philosophically, he is a naturalist who believes that there is no evidence of supernatural entities, so he looks for natural explanations for all things and believes that human thought is solely the product of physical processes in the human brain.[1] His research explores how the brain functions and how its uniquely human modes of thought developed through the process of evolution.

Pinker's views often dovetail with modern scientific atheists such as Richard Dawkins and Daniel Dennett. These authors see belief in God and the spiritual realm as a delusion created as a by-product of evolutionarily useful adaptations, but also as particularly problematic in the modern world. While these authors agree on many points, and any of them would have been a worthy subject for a chapter in this book, Pinker has explicitly developed a richer, fuller picture of the world and human nature in his writings, including views on how we developed language, morality, intelligence, and many of the traits that we associate with being human.

---

1. *Naturalist* is a philosophical position that became popular in America in the early twentieth century as a way to bridge science and philosophy. It indicates a belief that "reality is exhausted by nature, containing nothing 'supernatural,' and that the scientific method should be used to investigate all areas of reality, including the 'human spirit'" (Papineau, "Naturalism").

What Is real?

Science can potentially study anything that exists, our universe and everything in it, seeking to understand the causes of phenomena and the rules that govern the interactions of matter. We presume that both you the reader and we the authors of this book are of the species *Homo sapiens*, one of the millions of species of life that have evolved on the planet Earth, which circles a star in the Milky Way galaxy, one of a currently unknown number of galaxies strewn across the universe. The universe began fourteen billion years ago in what is called the Big Bang. As the universe expanded out from a single point it cooled, and matter, time, and the laws of nature distilled out. As it expanded and cooled further, galaxies were formed and our Sun and its planets came to exist. Life began on Earth perhaps four billion years ago when some organic compounds developed the ability to replicate. Life developed in the Earth's oceans slowly at first, through various kinds of single-celled organisms. Multicellular organisms of sufficient diversity to leave a discernible fossilized record developed about half a billion years ago. Life eventually crawled out of the ocean on to dry land, continuing its diversification. While many simpler life forms continued, more complex forms also evolved.

Figure 3.1: *March of Progress*, a popular icon of evolution originally appearing in *Early Man* by Time-Life Books.

Species evolve when breeding populations reproduce generations that have small random variations. If a particular variation affords an organism a better ability to survive and reproduce, over time it will begin to predominate in the population, a process called natural selection. Slowly, over millions of years and tens of thousands of generations, this process can give rise to more complex organisms with novel abilities. Even though we have no record of writing dating back more than six thousand years, individuals of our species developed the genetic ability to speak, read, and write about a million years ago in proto-humans who were slightly genetically different from modern humans. *Homo sapiens* have been around only about two hundred thousand years. Having been produced by a long process of evolution, *Homo sapiens* have a complex amalgam of traits that were naturally selected for many different reasons. The traits that we identify as distinctly human, such as our large brain that allows for language and introspection, developed over the past million years on the savannas of Africa as *Homo sapiens* lived in small bands of hunter-gatherers. These abilities must have given us an evolutionary advantage in that context.

A Picture

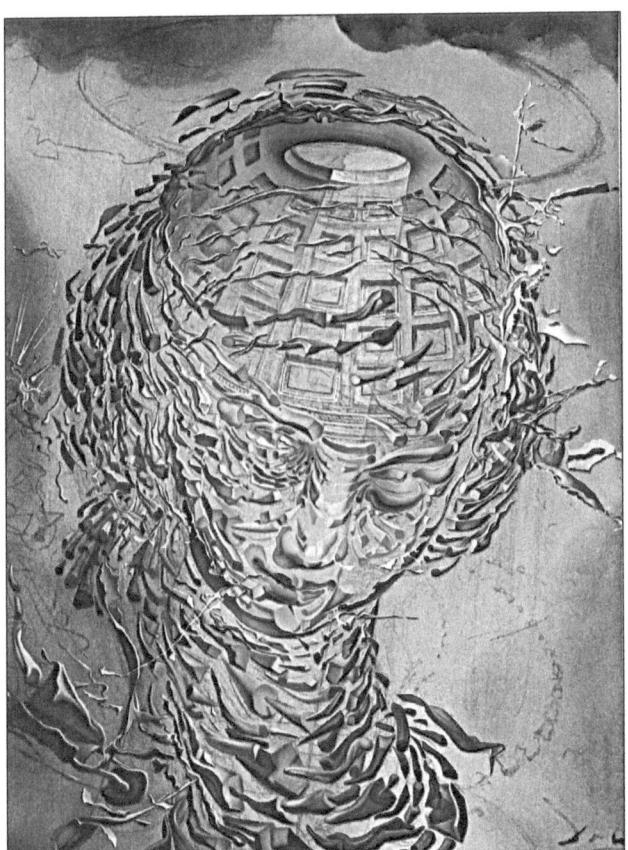

Figure 3.2: *Exploding Raphaelesque Head* by Salvador Dali.

Figure 3.2 shows a painting by Salvador Dali entitled *Exploding Raphaelesque Head*. It was used on the cover of Steven Pinker's book on human nature, *The Blank Slate*, and it is a good visual metaphor of his view of the human person as created by evolution. The painting depicts a swirling array of objects that have been repurposed to create a bust with a face reminiscent of the Madonna in a famous Renaissance painting by Raphael.

We have been created by evolution with many overlapping subsystems that perform various functions. These systems, some of which were originally developed for one purpose but eventually took on a new function, interact in complex ways to create what we know as human nature. Everything that we think of as uniquely human has arisen through the process of evolution to confer on our ancestors some advantage in reproduction over their rivals. We have been shaped by this process to respond to the world in certain characteristic ways. First among these uniquely human characteristics is the ability to think about and reshape our environment.

Knowledge and Understanding

In the *Exploding Raphaelesque Head* the Pantheon of Rome appears as the top of the Madonna's head complete with its oculus to let in light. You can see the dome from the inside because, of course, you can see the exploded head from the inside and the outside. Part of any human person is structured, like the Pantheon, and part is in flux, changing from person to person and moment to moment. In the painting, the part that is structured is our skull, which holds our brain, the seat of our thinking. As the light enters and fills the Pantheon through the oculus, ideas from the outside world enter and fill our brains in a particular, structured way. The process of evolution has shaped our brains so that they respond to the outside world in specific ways that increased our ability to survive and reproduce as hunter-gatherers on the savannas of Africa. In the painting there is no hard distinction between the inside and the outside of the Madonna. Her surface is permeable and her inside and outside are equal spaces. In the same way, there is no fundamental difference between what goes on in our heads and what goes on in the outside world—it is all just chemical reactions that obey the same physical laws of nature. Our thinking is not some fundamentally different sort of process than other processes in the world.

Homo sapiens are intelligent. They have the ability to create and work with concepts that match the world around us.[2] Thinking is done with our brains, which have the ability to create concepts by encoding information about the world through configuring bits of matter inside our brains based on input from our sense organs. Our brains can think by processing this information through manipulating these configured bits of matter to interact with other encoded bits of matter in structured ways. Together, this allows us to create concepts and manipulate them in order to create new concepts and beliefs in an almost unbounded manner.

Our brains do not come without a cost. They consume a lot of energy. The process of natural selection favors the development of such a costly organ only if it provides a benefit to the propagation of the species greater than the cost. We developed our large brains on the plains of Africa over the last few millions years through the coevolution of cognition, language, and sociality.[3] Developments in our brains allowed us to reason about the causal structure of the world, to use language and the rules of grammar to communicate this knowledge to others, and to negotiate and coordinate our activities with other human beings. This opened up a cognitive niche where humans could flourish by working together to intelligently and collaboratively overcome the defenses of plants and other animals, giving them a great advantage in speed of adaptation.

The mechanism of natural selection produces a slow arms race where one species adapts to prey upon another species, which then adapts better defenses and so on. This process typically unfolds over thousands of generations, as random variations in the population get slowly selected as advantageous to survival and propagation. However, humans have developed an ability to create mental models of the world and use cause and effect reasoning to learn how to defeat the defenses of their prey in the time-scale of a single lifetime. Humans can also convey this knowledge to other humans through the use of language, allowing them to coordinate activities so that many individuals could act together as one super organism and pass along their knowledge to their progeny. They can thus adapt over a single lifetime and pass this adaptation along to future generations, whereas their prey or enemies relying on natural selection can only adapt slowly over many generations. This is a substantial advantage for a species of hunter-gatherers.

2. Pinker, *How the Mind Works*, 24.
3. Pinker, "Cognitive Niche," 8993.

The process of natural selection has provided *Homo sapiens* with specific cognitive and linguistic abilities that are broadly shared and apparent across cultures and throughout time. Humans intuitively believe that living things have an invisible essence that gives them their form and powers.[4] Such beliefs allowed pre-scientific humans to make medicine from plants and animals, and to avoid things that would make them sick such as rotting meat, feces, and other people who were sick. But it also leads us to believe in sympathetic magic, for instance that eating or wearing a part of a fierce animal will make us fierce, and that "natural" foods are healthier than "artificial" foods. Humans intuitively believe in the persistence of objects in time and have a mental representation of where things are in the world and in relation to their own bodies.[5] Humans keep track of how objects move, fall, and bounce, attributing their motion to general laws. Humans have the mental ability to represent objects, their properties, and the laws that govern them with ideas, and we can combine ideas with such causal operators as *and, or, not, all, some, necessary, possible,* and *cause* in order to infer new ideas.[6] All of this confers an advantage in hunting and escaping from being hunted in an almost limitless variety of situations. *Homo sapiens* have an innate linguistic ability shared across the species, and manifested in many different languages.[7] The rules of grammar allow us to arbitrarily assign concepts to words, combine words into meaningful phrases about who did what to whom, where things are, and what is true about them, and then combine these phrases in arbitrary hierarchical combinations in a functionally infinite way to communicate our thoughts to others. We can distinguish between "dog bites man," "man bites dog," "man wonders if dog bites," and "man bites man-biting dog." This linguistic ability allows us to coordinate efforts and thinking with others and to pass along to others and the next generation what we have learned.

Our cognition, language, and sociality all rely on uniquely human qualities of our brain, and these qualities do not need to function perfectly in order to provide an evolutionary advantage. At first, our ability to reason simply had to allow early hominids to be marginally better predators and/or survivors than other species without these abilities. Over time there would be a selection pressure within hominids toward more sophisticated

---

4. Pinker, *Blank Slate*, 230.
5. Pinker, *Blank Slate*, 219–20.
6. Pinker, *Blank Slate*, 221.
7. Pinker, "Cognitive Niche," 8995.

reasoning, which would support more sophisticated hunting and survival strategies. *Homo sapiens* thus have a fine-tuned and innate ability to reason about the world as encountered on the African savanna. Our knowledge of the world, which gives us an advantage over other species, is related to the world outside of us by the structures of our senses and our brains. To say that we *know* the world around us means that we have encoded in our brains enough concepts derived from the world to allow us to reason successfully about it. We can get this knowledge from our own direct experience of the world, from others through the use of language, or from reasoning about data obtained from either of these sources.

The ability to work with concepts and language has also given us the ability for abstract reasoning in which we apply concepts learned in one concrete context to other, more abstract realms.[8] This can be seen in our use of language. I could, for instance, force a door open, force someone to answer my question, or force myself to behave responsibly. The first example is a concrete use of physical force. The second use of force, forcing someone to answer a question, is analogous to a physical force but it operates in the realm of interpersonal dynamics. The third example, forcing myself, implies a further abstraction into the realm of introspection, where something akin to the interaction of two people happens within myself. These examples show how we apply what we learn in one area to situations in other areas that have analogous causes. I see that I had to force the door to open, and I could reason that if I had not forced the door, it would still be closed. Then, sensing resistance in myself and thinking analogously, I might infer that if I do not force myself I will not behave responsibly.

The best way to acquire new knowledge of the world is through communicating with others in a process of conjecture and refutation, where we make conjectures about the world, test them, and allow ourselves and others to refute the ones that are false.[9] All other methods, including divine revelation, authority, and personal intuition, are prone to error and should be discarded. The scientific method of using conjecture and refutation to establish facts about the world and then developing theories that explain these facts and make testable predictions, and then performing experiments to verify or refute these predictions is the basis of all of the techno-

---

8. Pinker, "Cognitive Niche," 8997.

9. Pinker, "Three Reasons." Also, knowing that we can never rest in our knowledge, that it can never be sure, Pinker adds, "The beloved convictions of every time and culture may be decisively falsified, doubtless including some we hold today."

logical advances we have made in the last five hundred years. It is the best method to find out the truth about the world in which we live.

We estimate that the universe was created in the Big Bang fourteen billion years ago. If at some point in the future new data causes us to change this estimate significantly or if we were to abandon our understanding of the origin of the universe in a Big Bang in favor of a Little Swirly, we would be using the scientific method, not abandoning it. This does not mean that the scientific method yields arbitrary or necessarily tenuous results. At any moment, a scientific theory needs to be backed up with data that can be verified by independent researchers and subject to peer review in order to be considered true. *True* means the ability to explain data from past experiments and to predict future results. A theory is true if it does this well, and it becomes more sure as it makes more predictions that pass more tests. Disputes among rival theories are resolved by deciding which explains the data better, regardless of personal opinions or historical precedence. This is why modern science has been so effective at cutting through the layers of superstitious beliefs of the past. There are no beliefs too sacred to question and put to a scientific test, and we expect our understanding to grow and change as time progresses. Any particular belief that we have at this moment might be refuted in the future, and the most secure knowledge we have today comes from the conjectures that have withstood the most refutations. Newtonian physics were supplanted by quantum physics at one end of the spectrum and Einstein's theory of relativity at the other. But this does not make Newtonian physics *false*. Newtonian physics is true in a qualified sense. Newtonian physics is still used in making bridges and engines and most of the things of our day-to-day life. It simply has its limits and will not yield valid results when sizes are on the level of atoms or velocities begin to approach the speed of light.

Emotions and Morality

We can find better moral laws to guide our lives by using this same method of open debate. We can propose moral principles and give reasons for them, and if they convince others, they will be adopted. The Golden Rule is fundamental to any rational morality: do unto others, as you would have them do unto you.[10] We have no grounds for privileging our own interests over

---

10. For a short presentation on the fundamentals of morality see Pinker, "Steven Pinker Defines Morality."

the interests of others, so any moral laws need to bind others and ourselves equally. Appeals to faith or supernatural revelations are not a good basis of morality because they do not convince the skeptic.

Our moral theories are not completely flexible or arbitrary. Because of the cognitive niche in which we developed morals and emotions, we have certain moral propensities. *Homo sapiens* have a complex social nature that facilitates collaboration. Many species exhibit symbiotic altruism, where the actions of one individual directly benefit another individual while pursuing its own interests, as when a bird sits on the back of a large mammal and eats the ticks that are living on it.[11] Humans exhibit this sort of altruism in friendships based on shared interests and in parents collaborating to rear their biological children. Parents might sacrifice themselves for the benefit of their own children or for the benefit of the other parent who would then better ensure the survival of the next generation. Genes that favor such behavior will be selected for by evolution in any species as long as the benefit to the recipients, such as the survival of the offspring, is greater than the cost sustained by the one who sacrifices, discounted by their degree of relatedness.

Unlike most other species, humans also have developed a more sophisticated form of altruism where they help non-relatives so that these non-relatives can help them in the future.[12] Reciprocal altruism requires a number of cognitive features to function, such as the ability to recognize individuals, interpret their actions in relation to their competence, judge their sincerity and willingness to reciprocate, and recall and use this information appropriately in future decisions. Reciprocal altruism also requires a set of innate moral emotions such as sympathy and trust to extend the first favor; gratitude, loyalty, guilt, and shame to move individuals to repay favors; and anger and shame to move individuals to punish those who betray reciprocal debts. Because of our linguistic ability people can share their evaluation of the trustworthiness and competence of individuals with others, creating the possibility of a reputation that would need to be burnished and protected.

Through the process of natural selection over hundreds of thousands of years, *Homo sapiens* developed the emotions of sympathy, gratitude, loyalty, guilt, shame, anger, and a sense of justice because they were advantageous for our survival by fostering reciprocal altruism. Reciprocal

11. Pinker, "Cognitive Niche," 8994; Pinker, *Blank Slate*, 242–43.
12. Pinker, *Blank Slate*, 243–44.

altruism can evolve in a species that has intelligence because it benefits all of the participants. Those who try to cheat will eventually be found out and shunned or otherwise punished. Those who participate do so willingly, not by explicitly calculating their advantage in any particular altruistic action, but as their emotions, shaped by the forces of natural selection, lead them to enjoy altruistic behavior. Emotions are the basis of the alliances and friendships that bind a community for the benefit of all, and they are the basis of a natural morality.

Reciprocal altruism generates different prescribed social interactions within and among different societies, but within each society, social norms have moral content. There are four different relational models governing four different social situations.[13] First, families and groups that are seen as "one flesh" operate on a Communal Sharing model, where all resources are shared by members without keeping score. The group is typically built up by bodily contact, communal meals, and shared emotional experiences, and has to be safeguarded against contamination. Communal Sharing evolved from maternal care and mutualism and is regulated in our brains through the chemical oxytocin, which is naturally released in nursing mothers and calms and comforts a person. Second, Authority Ranking governs the interactions of hierarchically defined relationships where superiors receive tribute from inferiors in exchange for protection. It evolved from primate dominance hierarchies and is regulated at least in part by testosterone-sensitive circuits in our brains. Third, Equality Matching governs reciprocal relationships among equals and involves keeping track of complex exchanges of goods and services to ensuring fair exchange and cementing relationships among neighbors, colleagues, and acquaintances. It involves many parts of our brain that developed because of the Cognitive Niche to register intentions, calculations, cheating, and conflict. Fourth, information technologies, literacy, and facilities with numbers and accounting has allowed for a new kind of relationship that governs modern societies—Market Pricing—which sets prices, salaries, benefits, interests, and other aspects of the modern world. Rather than being based in specific evolutionary advances, Market Pricing developed intentionally and rationally as societies grew larger as a good way to manage the interactions of millions of people.

---

13. Pinker, *Better Angels*, 625–28. Here Pinker is following the theories of anthropologist Alan Fiske.

In any society everyday morality is not based on explicit calculations of the Golden Rule, but on respecting the social norms embodied in these relational models.[14] People are expected to act in accord with these social norms and are judged as morally deficient if they act against them. These norms are very situational, with expectations depending upon a particular relational model, the social roles of participants, the social context of the event, and the particular resources being shared. For instance, dining at a restaurant involves a Market Pricing model of sharing. Imagine a person at the end of the meal invoking a Communal Sharing model by thanking the restaurateur and offering to have her over for supper in the future. The diner would either be considered woefully deficient in understanding and deserving of a good "talking to" or sufficiently morally deficient to justify turning over to the police. Similarly, a person who took out at a wallet at the end of a dinner party to pay the host for the meal would be judged as either obtuse or offensive. If the community considered the resource under consideration *sacred*, the offense would be considered grave. "If someone offered to purchase your child (suddenly thrusting a Communal Sharing relationship under the light of Market Pricing), you would not ask how much he was offering but would be offended at the very idea." If you responded with anything less than indignation, you would be judged as morally deficient for even considering the idea.

While scientific discoveries increasingly explain the evolutionary roots of morality and the factors that impinge upon individual moral decisions, they do not take away individual responsibility in decision-making. There is still "the mysterious notion of uncaused causation that underlies the will" and makes it free.[15] Any of the scientific methods that predict human choice are never more than probable, and do not compel a specific choice. This freedom cannot be explained by random neural events or chaos theory, and it is the foundation that makes ethics possible:

> Science and ethics are two self-contained systems played out among the same entities in the world, just as poker and bridge are different games played with the same fifty-two-card deck. The science game treats people as material objects, and its rules are the physical processes that cause behavior through natural selection and neurophysiology. The ethics game treats people as equivalent, sentient, rational, free-willed agents, and its rules are the calculus

---

14. Pinker, *Better Angels*, 628–30.
15. Pinker, *How the Mind Works*, 54–56.

that assigns moral value to behavior through the behavior's inherent nature or its consequences.

Science and morality are two different ways of conceptualizing human beings for different purposes. We are free to choose one conceptualization over the other depending on what we are trying to evaluate, just as we can also conceptualize people as taxpayers "and two hundred pounds of ballast on a commuter airplane, depending on the purpose of the discussion." Such simplifications allow us to more readily investigate different aspects of humanity. They also allow us to investigate the brain as an information processing system without implying that people are robots.

The More Ephemeral Things of Life

Though human nature has been created through the process of evolution, humans seem to spend an inordinate amount of time pursuing activities that do not contribute to our reproductive success:

> In all cultures, people tell stories and recite poetry. They joke, laugh, and tease. They sing and dance. They decorate surfaces. They perform rituals. They wonder about the causes of fortune and misfortune, and hold beliefs about the supernatural that contradict everything else they know about the world. They concoct theories of the universe and their place within it.[16]

All of these uniquely human activities rely on tapping into our pleasure centers in ways that shortcut the usual routes that developed to serve particular purposes, hijacking abilities that were developed because they led to actual reproductive advantage. For example, cheesecake tastes so good because it taps directly into "circuits that gave us trickles of enjoyment from the sweet taste of ripe fruit, the creamy mouth feel of fats and oils from nuts and meat, and the coolness of fresh water" (525). Our taste buds developed a preference for fresh fruit and meats, and we developed cheesecake to exploit this and give us a mega-dose of pleasure without fruit or meat. In the same way, people tell stories because they deliver "a simulation of life that an audience can enter in the comfort of their cave, couch, or theater seat.

---

16. Pinker, *How the Mind Works*, 521. This section presents Pinker's explanation of this important insight, which is found in the last chapter of *How the Mind Works*. In this section, instead of footnotes we will denote page references with parenthetical citations, all of which refer to page numbers in *How the Mind Works*.

Words can evoke mental images, which can activate the parts of the brain that register the world when we actually perceive it" (539). We love stories for the same reasons we love life. Perhaps people joke and tease as a form of play fighting as practice for the real thing (546). In this scenario, laughter comes about as a way to signal our mock opponent that their attack was effective while also acknowledging it as a sham. Being social animals, we have developed many ways of broadcasting our mental states in ways that are involuntary so that they are honest and cannot be faked. Joking and teasing also reinforce the social bonds on which we rely for survival. Singing, dancing, and visual arts tap into our innate abilities for language and image recognition and our system of motor control.

Religion is a more complex phenomenon. Rituals often have an important role in bonding the community for everyone's benefit. "Food taboos keep members of the tribe from becoming intimate with outsiders. Rites of passage demarcate the people who are entitled to the privileges of social categories (fetus or family member, child or adult, single or married) so as to preempt endless haggling over gray areas. Painful initiations weed out anyone who wants the benefits of membership without being committed to paying the costs" (555). But religion is also a "desperate measure that people resort to when the stakes are high and they have exhausted the usual techniques for the causation of success—medicines, strategies, courtship, and, in the case of the weather, nothing" (556). This is not completely irrational. "Religious concepts are human concepts with a few emendations that make them wondrous and a longer list of standard traits that make them sensible to our ordinary ways of knowing" (557). The emendations are just enough to offer the hope of success or an explanation of data that stymies our everyday theories, providing enough impetus for us to believe in what is "palpably not true" (554).

Beyond any of these activities lie our human propensity to ask questions that we cannot seem to answer, such as "where the universe came from, how physical flesh can give rise to sentient minds, why bad things happen to good people, [and] what happens to our thoughts and feelings when we die" (525). Our minds evolved in order to assist us with survival on the plains of Africa, giving us the ability to reason successfully about the objects of our everyday world such as animals, plants, weather, and the minds of other human beings. There is no reason to believe that we are equipped to understand arbitrary truths beyond those that are sufficiently similar to the ones that allowed us to survive. Even if these seemingly intractable questions have answers, the process of natural selection might not have equipped us with minds that could understand them. As the saying goes, if all you have is a hammer, every problem looks like a nail. In this light, religion and philosophy go so far astray because they "are in part the application of mental tools to problems they were not designed to solve." We cannot understand or explain away our sense of having a free will and a consciousness, a sense of self, but this does not justify making metaphysical or supernatural explanations to explain them. "Maybe philosophical problems are hard not because they are divine or irreducible or meaningless or workaday science, but because the mind of *Homo sapiens* lacks the cognitive equipment to solve them" (561). This is not to say something about the intrinsically difficult nature of the questions, it is an observation about human brains and their capabilities, "equivalent to observing that cats are color-blind or that monkeys cannot learn long division" (563).

Where Things Go Wrong

Our intrinsic ways of thinking, emoting, and moralizing, tuned as they are by a million years of evolution to a lifestyle of small bands of hunter-gatherers, do not always serve us well in contemporary situations. Humans have only lived settled lives in large cities since the domestication of plants and animals ten thousand years ago; too short a time for our genome to have significantly evolved through natural selection to adjust to this new situation. We still think using brains with mental processes that were tuned to deal with life on the savannas of Africa so our natural, intuitive ways of thinking can sometimes not fit our new life situations well. For instance, modern biology is of immense benefit to society, curing diseases and helping to produce more and better food, but to learn modern biology we must unlearn our innate view that living things have an intangible essence. Such beliefs served us well on the savannah one hundred thousand years ago, but they obscure the deeper reality that life is essentially chemical processes, which is the basis of progress in modern biology. Any recourse to immaterial essences as explanatory causes for biological phenomena obscures rather than clarifies our deeper understanding of the world. Our minds, which distinguish us from other animals, are not immaterial and they are not unified. Our minds are a complex system of biological processes that have developed over time, an array of specialized subprocesses that can be thought of as mental modules each dedicated to some specific task.[17] "Our moral intuitions aren't unified. We're often at war with ourselves. Different intuitions pull in different directions, and they probably do involve different circuits in the brain."[18]

Emotions that once served us well can become problematic. Loyalty to kin and to tribe, which bonded primitive bands of hunters, is also the basis of nepotism—the scourge of modern corporations and governments.[19] The emotion of disgust originally evolved to lead us to avoid biological contaminants such as sick people and spoiled food. It was then recruited by our moral sense to lead us to shun actions that break social contracts, go against taboos, or offend the sacred.[20] This is not irrational. For reciprocal altruism to work, we have to judge whether the person we are trusting is the kind of person who holds our relationship as sacrosanct as we do, or would betray us if given the chance. But holding certain ideas as sacrosanct so that they cannot even be questioned leads to making bad decisions. If we say that every human life is sacred, is it wrong to put a price on an individual's life? Hospitals do it every day when they make decisions about how to use their resources. Should they spend a million dollars on a liver transplant to try to save one child, or should they use the money for better diagnostic equipment that could potentially save thousands?[21] In a complex, modern society it seems necessary to ponder these questions even though they generate feelings of moral outrage and disgust, because we cannot trust our natural sense of moral outrage and disgust to necessarily point us to the best solution.

We can choose the best moral laws that should govern society through dialogue with one another only if we let the evidence of science guide our decisions. Our natural attractions and repulsions are one piece of the discussion, but they should not be allowed to entirely determine the outcome. We can decide where to draw the line between spending money on an expensive and heroic effort to save one child versus improving the lives of many children through the purchase of diagnostic equipment by studying the outcomes of many cases, quantifying their benefits, and agreeing on the most effective way to balance these competing goods.

17. Pinker, *How the Mind Works*, 27.
18. Pinker as quoted in Flatow, "Can Science."
19. Pinker, *Blank Slate*, 245.
20. For moral outrage, see also Pinker, *Better Angels*, 630.
21. Pinker, *Blank Slate*, 277–79.

Since we can use logic and learn from one another, we can construct a better morality for ourselves and use it to build a better society. This is already happening. Although it might not be intuitively obvious, society has become progressively less violent in recent centuries.[22] Despite the grand scale of notable failures, such as two world wars, the twentieth century was less violent than the nineteenth century, which was less violent than the eighteenth century. This holds true for almost all ways we might want to quantify it: deaths due to murder, war, or starvation as a percentage of the population, or statistics for crimes not resulting in death. As a society, we have expanded rights and freedoms accorded individuals, abolishing slavery and giving women the right to vote. We have done this as a society by choosing to live in accord with better moral principles. While racism and sexism are still problems in our society, we can combat them by choosing to do so for moral reasons.[23] It is intuitively obvious and scientifically verifiable that there are differences between the sexes and differences between the races. We can oppose sexism and racism not by denying these facts, but by asserting that it is wrong to judge any individual based on the demographics of a group to which they belong.[24] Thus, while it is true that men are, on average, stronger than women, we can say that it is wrong to bar all women from certain jobs because these jobs demand physical strength. The decision should be made based on whether a particular person, male or female, has the strength to do the job.

Pinker's Relationship to a Wider Tradition

In 2004, *Time* magazine named Steven Pinker as one of the one hundred most influential people in the world today. In 2013, *Prospect* magazine conducted a poll of the top "world thinkers" from a list of sixty-five people who had influenced the year's biggest questions in the previous

---

22. Pinker, *Better Angels*, 192–99.
23. Pinker, *Blank Slate*, 145–48.
24. Pinker also offers a caveat to this position. The prohibition against discrimination is applicable only where there is a significant amount of overlap in the demographics of different groups. For instance, we can agree that human children generally benefit from education and thus we can morally prescribe that they get it. An education might also be of benefit to some chimpanzees, but few would benefit, and it would be very expensive to figure out which ones. So it is morally acceptable not to give chimpanzees an education at public expense, while requiring it of human children (Pinker, *Blank Slate*, 148).

twelve months.[25] Pinker came in at number three. Beyond his considerable influence in society in general, Pinker's views are in close alignment with some of the most prominent scientific and philosophical atheists of day, such as Richard Dawkins and Daniel Dennett. To give a sense of this, in *How the Mind Works*, Pinker cites significant ideas of Dawkins eight times, nine times for Dennett, all of them positively except for one time when he calls Dennett's argument inconclusive.[26] Pinker also thanks them both in the introduction. Dennett cites Pinker twice in his book *Breaking the Spell: Religion as a Natural Phenomenon* and twice in *Consciousness Explained*. Dawkins cites Pinker's *How the Mind Works* and *The Blank Slate* in his book *The God Delusion*.

In *Prospect* magazine's poll of top world thinkers in which Pinker came in third, Dawkins was voted as the top world thinker. Dawkins is so revered among modern atheists that the Atheist Alliance of America has named their annual award after him, explaining: "The Richard Dawkins Award is given each year to honor an outstanding atheist whose contributions raise public awareness of the nontheist life stance; who, through writings, media, the arts, film, and/or the stage, advocates increased scientific knowledge; who, through work or by example, teaches acceptance of the nontheist philosophy; and whose public postures mirrors the uncompromising nontheist life stance of Dr. Richard Dawkins."[27] It was awarded to Daniel Dennett in 2007 and to Steven Pinker in 2013.[28]

Finally, in an interview with *The New York Times*, Richard Dawkins was asked who were his favorite contemporary writers and thinkers. He replied:

> I've already mentioned Dan Dennett. I'll add Steven Pinker, A. C. Grayling, Daniel Kahneman, Jared Diamond, Matt Ridley, Lawrence Krauss, Martin Rees, Jerry Coyne—indeed quite a few of the luminaries that grace the Edge online salon conducted by John Brockman (the Man with the Golden Address Book). All share the same honest commitment to real-world truth, and the belief that discovering it is the business of scientists—and philosophers who take the trouble to learn science. Many of these

25. Dugdale, "Richard Dawkins."

26. Citations of Dawkins beginning on pages 36, 44, 133, 155, 208, 314, 397, and 402. Citations of Dennett beginning on pages 14, 54, 79, 98, 133, 144, 147, 165, and 328.

27. Atheist Alliance of America, "Richard Dawkins Award."

28. See Dawkins's commentary on Pinker receiving the award at Dawkins, "Steven Pinker."

"Third Culture" thinkers write very well. (Why is the Nobel Prize in Literature almost always given to a novelist, never a scientist? Why should we prefer our literature to be about things that didn't happen? Wouldn't, say, Steven Pinker be a good candidate for the literature prize?)[29]

Steven Pinker is a central theorist for an influential group of atheist scientists who share ideas in developing a coherent, progressive, naturalist explanation of life, the universe, and everything.

---

29. *New York Times*, "Richard Dawkins."

4

In Comparison

The three previous chapters have explored three very different pictures of the world, the Christian picture of Thomas Aquinas, the Buddhist picture of Tsongkhapa, and the modern naturalist picture of Steven Pinker. Each of these pictures was presented in its own terms, without explicit reference to other viewpoints, but in truth each picture implicitly challenges the validity of alternative views. In this chapter we will look at some of these contrasts as they touch on fundamental areas of philosophy such as how we know what is real, true, and good.

The subjects dealt with in this chapter are more narrowly focused than the broad pictures we dealt with in the first three chapters. Some of the material will be a retelling of what was learned previously, put in a new context for comparison. But new information will be added to fill in the details of particular comparisons, often from other scholars who have appropriated the tradition laid out by our primary authors and see themselves following their footsteps.

The Human Person

The view of the human person differs radically among our three authors. Since it is central to understanding each of the world-pictures, it is woven throughout the fabric of each of the previous chapters. To orient the comparisons to come, let us begin by highlighting and comparing each author's main points.

Steven Pinker sees the human person as the product of evolution, a living organism that has evolved an ability to use concepts and language in order to successfully collaborate with other hominoids to flourish on the plains of Africa between four million and one hundred thousand years ago.[1] We subsequently spread out from there to successfully colonize the rest of land on our planet. Our thinking and knowing are the result of material processes centered mostly in our brains. Our thinking happens through the complex interactions of neurons within our brains, and our knowing somehow involves chemical and structural changes within our central nervous system. We are just beginning to understand how this works, so the details are still unknown, but we are making headway that seems to confirm these hypotheses.

Within an organism our development is guided by our genetic make-up subject to a certain amount of random fluctuations and environmental conditions. Once an egg is fertilized by a sperm we have our genetic content specified, and the cells start to divide and replicate. But there is no unity to this new collection of cells for a while until it reaches a critical level. At that point, organization happens and cells begin to specialize within an overall plan, functioning as a whole. As the embryo develops, it gains various abilities. On the other end of life, there is also no clear threshold for death. The various systems and organs that make up a person begin to break down at different times, eventually losing their symbiotic relationships to the whole until a functional unity is completely gone. At that point, the person is gone, and the chemicals from which the person was made quickly begin to lose their organization.

Thomas Aquinas sees the human person as body/soul composite, made by God in order to share God's overflowing love and joy. Our ultimate destiny is to join God in heaven. Modern Thomists generally believe that science can best explain the creation of our bodies, and so would agree with Pinker on the evolution of our bodies. However, they insist that our souls are individually created by God, as they not only inform our bodies, but they have a substantial immaterial aspect as well. This immaterial aspect is shown in our ability to know and understand, abilities that are beyond the capabilities of matter.

Aquinas speculated that a developing fetus went through a series of souls as it gradually gained the material sophistication to support more complex life forms, with God finally creating the human soul when it was

---

1. Pinker, *How the Mind Works*, 201. This date corresponds with the appearance of australopithecines, the first human ancestors to walk upright and live on the savannah through the time when *Homo sapiens* began migrating out of Africa.

sufficiently developed to support rationality.² At the end of life, there comes a point when the body loses its ability to remain united to the soul. But the soul, having an aspect that is also immaterial and substantial, cannot be destroyed through physical processes, so it remains in existence, separated from its body, which dies.³ Through God's action we can gain new bodies, which are not like our former, corruptible ones, and enter a new, eternal life in heaven. We are also free to refuse the gift of joining God in heaven and enter hell, an existence of torment bereft of all joy and love, since joy and love are of God.

Tsongkhapa sees all sentient life as caught in a beginningless and recurring cycle of suffering known as samsara. Our own ignorance of this fact interacts with the laws of karma to cause us to be reborn time and again into lives that are ultimately unsatisfying. We can be reborn not simply as humans. There are six realms of different types of sentient beings into which we could reincarnate—human, semi-divine, divine, animal, hungry ghost, and hell beings. Through a process of meditation and philosophical analysis we can overcome our delusion and break this cycle of rebirth, becoming enlightened. Enlightenment is beyond conception and thus beyond words, since words and concepts apply to the realm of samsara. While we are trapped in samsara, the laws of physics and science apply to us but they do not apply to enlightenment. Thus, there can be rapprochement between Buddhism and science on the mundane truths of this world, but Buddhism

---

2. Aquinas's text reads: "Therefore it must be said that the intellective soul is created by God at the completion of man's coming-into-being. This soul is at one at the same time both a sensitive and nutritive life-principle, the preceding forms having been dissolved" (Aquinas, *Summa Theologiae*, 1:118.2 resp. 2). We are asserting the consensus opinion of Aquinas's own view, but it is a contentious point in modern Thomism since it is often used to place Aquinas in opposition to contemporary Catholic teachings that individual human life begins at conception. For instance, Jason Eberl argues that Aquinas believed the development of the fetus was guided from without by the seminal fluid, but since we now know that it is guided from within by each cell's own DNA, following Aquinas's logic, we should conclude differently than he did, that the new life should be considered to have a rational soul when it is either "a one-celled zygote—the immediate product of conception—or an early embryo—formed approximately two weeks after conception" (Eberl, "Aquinas's Account," 392). More radically, Melissa Rovig Vanden Bout "advances a different interpretation of Aquinas's views: that the embryo, even before the advent of the rational soul, is human" (Vanden Bout, "Thomas Aquinas," abstract). Vanden Bout argues that although Aquinas did not address this question directly, any other interpretation would lead to untenable contradictions in his thought that he would have found unacceptable.

3. Aquinas, *Summa Theologiae*, 1:75.6.

holds that there is a much larger reality than what we see around us every day. As there is no beginning to samsara nor to individual mind-streams, there is no creator God or absolute time of creation.

What Is Real? How Do We Know?

What is real, and how do we know? Are we to trust our senses to tell us about the world we live in, or is there a deeper truth hidden from our senses but available to us through thought, or meditation, or prayer, or science? Is everything that we see an illusion, as if we were in a dream, and if so, how would we know?

When we are dreaming, we usually don't notice we are dreaming. We pay attention to the dream, and the experience seems real until we wake up and realize that we had been dreaming. Tsongkhapa believed that all of our ordinary experiences of the world were like a dream because the world lacked the substance and givenness that we normally attributed to it.[4] Reality as presented by experience is illusory, it has maya. It fools us into thinking that it has a giveness that it lacks in reality, and we are trapped in this delusion. This does not have to be taken on faith. Meditation techniques, common to Buddhists and Hindus, have been developed to clear one's mind and focus one's attention. When these techniques are used to examine the contents of one's own awareness, one comes to see first hand that there are experiences but no experiencer experiencing them. It is our reification of our self that keeps us bound to this dream. Once we see that there is no self, the dream begins to unravel. Then we can begin to see that the mundane world of our senses lacks the reality and solidity that we formerly ascribed to it, and we will see that this deeper reality is so different from ordinary experience that words, concepts, and reasoning learned from mundane experience cannot be used to describe it. It is thus beyond the ability of words and concepts to describe, but it is not beyond our ability to experience.

For Tsongkhapa, enlightenment is not an all or nothing state. Enlightenment can be attained in levels or degrees. It can be glimpsed in moments of meditation, confirming that one is on the right path. Through study and meditation, guided by an experienced master who has already achieved a certain level of enlightenment, one can slowly deepen and extend these periods of clarity. We cannot begin down this path to deeper knowledge unless

---

4. Tsongkhapa, *Great Treatise*, 2:116.

we allow ourselves to question the apparent givenness of reality. Often these helpful doubts arise because of our dissatisfaction with life.

In comparison, Thomas Aquinas also believes that the physical world of our experience is not the deepest reality. God is the deepest reality. God is reality itself, and the physical world exists in dependence upon God. The world exists because God holds it in existence. Unlike Tsongkhapa, Aquinas does not believe that this world is a dream we need to wake up from nor an illusion we need to get beyond. Since God intentionally made the world and put us in it in order to share his love, we encounter God, the ultimate reality, through a deeper appropriation of our experiences of this world. The world as we experience it may not be ultimate, in the sense of self-existent, but it has an existence of its own, derived but still real.

For Aquinas, we primarily find truth through our bodies and the experiences of our senses. While God, as truth itself, has the nature of that which is most knowable, human beings were made to know the things of this world and can only come to know God through God's effects in this world and through extrapolation from this world.[5] Since learning is fraught with problems and requires great effort, God has also augmented our learning by revealing things that are important for us to know. This process culminates in a direct vision of God, which requires an additional grace that lifts us beyond our natural abilities. This grace will allow us to have a new life in heaven, where we will see God "as he is," but even in heaven we will have bodies—newly made, more perfect than our earthly bodies, but we will still be embodied. We come to know the world around us and the things in it through a process of abstraction. Our understanding can be faulty, but it is best corrected through logical analysis and further experiences, guided by divine revelation, rather than finding truth through some other means such as deep meditation.

Steven Pinker believes that we can only encounter reality through our senses. Our senses give us information about the physical world, and we have no indications to warrant belief in a supernatural reality beyond the physical world in which we live. The physical world is real and putative—spiritual realms are not. Talk of religion, spiritual realms, and divine beings is simply a holdover from our superstitious past. Such beliefs arise because of the ways our brains evolved to respond to life on the savannas of Africa. Religious beliefs were once innocuous and perhaps even helpful at bonding a community together, but now they get in the way of a deeper,

---

5. Turner, *Thomas Aquinas*, 52–54.

scientific understanding of reality. Reality is best understood through the application of the scientific method, proposing hypotheses, rigorously testing them, and then using that data to form theories about the world and testing those theories.

Pinker believes that our ability to know the world is limited and can be led astray by our natural abilities as they are brought to bear on situations that are different than those which guided their development during our evolution.[6] Our senses and our minds were tuned by evolution to enhance our survival on the plains of Africa.[7] We can predominantly see wavelengths of light that come from the sun and reflect off of the ordinary objects on the surface of planet Earth. We cannot see radio waves, which are electromagnetic waves just like sunlight, but at a different frequency. Our sense of touch is calibrated to the level of granularity encountered on the plains of Africa. A ruler seems to have a straight edge, even though it is not straight on a microscopic level. More importantly, our brains, rather than being unified general information processing systems, contain a number of specific subsystems to deal with different aspects of the world.[8] We have a specific cognitive faculty of intuitive physics for dealing with how objects move and bend and persist in time. We have another cognitive faculty of intuitive biology that deals with living objects. "Its core intuition is that living things house an essence that gives them their form and powers and drives their growth and bodily functions." Once we categorize objects as living, we think about their movements differently than we do inanimate objects. Modern biology seeks to uncover the chemical basis of life, which requires abandoning a belief in vital essences and unlearning our innate intuitive biology. Humans have an innate cognitive faculty of intuitive engineering that pictures tools as objects designed for a specific purpose, and it must be unlearned in order to learn the modern science of evolution in which the dynamics of natural selection of random variations replaces purposeful design. If we think of species as designed, we will look for a designer and a purpose. The modern theory of evolution allows for neither a design nor a designer to explain the creation of complex organisms. Humans have an innate, intuitive psychology that attributes the behavior of other people to beliefs and desires that are contained in an invisible entity we call their mind or soul. This has historically served humanity well, leading us to respect

6. Pinker, *Blank Slate*, 239–40.
7. See also Pinker, *Blank Slate*, 197.
8. Pinker, *Blank Slate*, 219–22.

the rights of other living people and to treat them quite differently than we would treat a dead human body or a living tree. But modern neurobiology is showing that the physical brain is the center of our reasoning, knowing, and willing—no soul required.

Pinker holds that belief in a soul leads to binary thinking about life and the mind that is untenable. In reality, there is no distinct line between life and non-life or mind and non-mind. Life and mind emerge gradually from tissues growing from a single cell. Any attempt to set hard and fast boundaries can be met by ambiguous cases that defy classification. For instance, some might look to the moment of conception as the time when new life begins and a new soul created. But there is no moment of conception. When a sperm enters an egg it takes a day or more for the chromosomes to combine. In the meantime, other sperm might have entered the egg and it takes time to eject the extra chromosomes, from 24 to 48 hours. As the new cell begins to divide, it might become a new baby, but in the next several days it also might split into identical twins or triplets, or more likely than not, be spontaneously aborted. There is no moment for this ensoulment to happen. In a further example, if human cloning becomes possible, which looks likely, any single human cell could be grown into a new person. When would this new person get a new soul? These are just a few examples of how our intuitive ways of understanding the world, which served us well when we were hunter-gatherers on the plains of Africa, can lead us astray when we try to understand the deeper reality of the world.

According to Aquinas, human individuals are body/soul composites, not souls inhabiting bodies, nor bodies without souls. Our intellectual ability reveals that there is an underlying immaterial aspect to our souls.[9] Knowledge as such cannot be material, or our knowledge would have material constraints that it seems to lack. Our bodies do not give rise to our souls, nor could they, since our souls have something immaterial and subsistent about them. Each human soul is created directly by God, and it is the soul's existence that is the basis of our existence as body-soul composites. When our bodies die, since our souls have an immaterial aspect as well, they do not cease to exist.[10] Material corruption cannot destroy them. But our souls retain an orientation toward having a body, and we are made complete again in heaven through receiving new bodies.

---

9. Aquinas, *Summa Theologiae*, 1:75.2. Explained in chapter 1, pp. 13–14.
10. Aquinas, *Summa Theologiae*, 1:75.6.

Aquinas believed that human beings were created and existed as individuals, understood as individuals, and lived eternally in the afterlife as individuals. In contrast, Tsongkhapa taught that our confusion was individual and must be dealt with on an individual basis, but that the enlightened buddha-mind was singular and shared by all. Our confusion and the karmic dirt created by our individual histories is a unique cover hiding the one buddha-nature at the core of every sentient being.

In Aquinas's day there was no consensus about what constituted an individual person. There were some who believed that understanding was shared, with all people participating in different degrees in a common, universal mind. Aquinas rejected this as counter to our experience of individually attaining knowledge through our own effort and only having access to our own thoughts. There were others in Aquinas's day who thought that individuals each had a number of different souls with no overarching, single soul controlling the rest. For instance, some thought that humans had a vegetative soul that governed nutrition, an animal soul that governed locomotion, and an intellectual soul that governed our understanding. Aquinas rejected this scenario as being insufficient to explain our unity. Individuals must each have one overarching substantial form that is the basis of each person's individual existence, or we would not each be a unified whole.

Tsongkhapa believed that the evidence pointed in the opposite direction. He taught that our unexamined experience indeed leads us to see the reality of individuality as a given fact, but saw this as a symptom of our delusion rather than a hallmark of lucidity. Philosophical analysis coupled with pointed meditation could help us see through this delusion. We are not a unified whole, we only appear to be one. In reality, we are composed of five *skandhas*—body, sensations, mental processes, habits/memories, and consciousness—each of which are constantly changing. The superposition of these five skandhas gives the impression of a fixed soul in which they adhere, an underlying unity. But there is no fixed soul that unifies the five skandhas, there are only the five skandhas, and even they do not exist ultimately.

Since there is no unifying principle, such as a soul, the person only exists nominally as a unified individual. Without unifying principles, there is no fixed boundary between various collections of skandhas, and no real separation between different individuals. There are apparent differences and functional differences between individuals, but there is no hard and fast separation of one person from another. Ultimately, just as souls do not exist, individual mind-streams do not exist, and the boundaries that separate us one from one another are provisional and illusory rather than real and fixed.

In a description of the night when the Buddha became enlightened, the modern Buddhist scholar Alan Wallace gives an explanation of how the Buddha used samadhi (focused meditation) to see through the delusion of our separate selves and perceive the laws of karma that govern rebirths, thus enabling him to see the path to liberation:

> Using the laser-sharp focus of samadhi, he penetrated through what we call the ordinary mind—the mind that is busy remembering, imagining, and desiring, *I want this, I don't want that*. He calmed that level of mind so that it became completely transparent, and he was able to tap into a deeper stratum of consciousness. Being very curious, he directed that very pure, focused attention back through his own life, and then back to previous lives, which manifested to him with complete clarity. Tapping into deep memory, he was able to recall an endless number of preceding lives and the circumstances of each life. As far back as he looked, he could never find a beginning. So he stopped looking, effectively saying, "I have enough data."
>
> He then expanded his vision, attending to other people's mind-streams, and he saw how their mind-streams, just like his own, seemed to recede endlessly. Then he did what we might call a meta-analysis, examining whether, in this stream of lifetimes, the behavior of one lifetime is related coherently and causally to the events of a later lifetime. He could see patterns: if this happens, then that happens; where this does not happen, that does not happen. He didn't speak of an underlying mechanism but rather of a phenomenological causality. From these observations, he came to certain principles or laws concerning samsara, which is what we call the cycling through one process of becoming after another, over and over again.
>
> All this took place in one night. It was a very good night. Finally he raised the question: What can bring samsara to an end? How can we free ourselves from being thrown compulsively and involuntarily from lifetime to lifetime? By morning, he saw how to accomplish the cessation of this cycle. He abandoned the very causes that perpetuate that cycle, and his mind was completely freed of all obscurations.[11]

---

11. Luisi, *Mind and Life*, 152. By "phenomenological causality," Wallace is referring to the phenomena of the basic experience of consciousness, and the cause and effect

This short passage ties together many Buddhist themes such as beginningless nescience, the reliance on direct experience and philosophical analysis rather than external authorities and theories, the pragmatic nature of Buddhism, and of course, our illusion of separateness from each other. It paints a very good Buddhist picture of the world and what we can hope to achieve ourselves.

Finally, we can ask where our basic ability to reason about the world came from. Buddhists hold that our human ability to reason, as distinct from our consciousness, which is beginningless, is a product of our karmic history. We have had many different incarnations, some in realms such as the animal realm, where we can experience pain and pleasure but with a very limited ability to reason. We now have a human birth because we are ready to use the abilities of logic that come along with being human. Ultimate truth is not logical, it does not obey the principle of noncontradiction and cannot be discovered through reason, but reason is powerful enough to cut through maya and expose the delusions we are living under, undermining wrong views. Words and concepts cannot describe ultimate reality, but they can describe mundane existence and expose its flaws.

Aquinas believes that God gave humanity the ability to reason so that we could know God and understand God's plan for the world, and in so doing we could love God more and live more in accord with God's plan. The constructs of logic reflect truth, and we were made to understand truth. Even God cannot contradict truth since God is truth itself. There are no contradictions in God. God is omnipotent, but God cannot do what is logically impossible, such as make a square circle or a perfect mistake. This would be contradictory. People have the natural ability to think logically because they were all made in the image of God, though some can do this more easily than others.

Pinker believes that *Homo sapiens* developed our cognitive ability as one of the parts of the cognitive niche that gave us an evolutionary advantage in the savannas of Africa beginning a million years ago. We developed an ability to use logic in constructing new knowledge because it was part of

---

relationships that we notice when we simply observe our experience of consciousness. Wallace believes that modern science cannot understand consciousness because it is constrained by the dictates of scientific materialism, which seeks to explain consciousness in terms of chemical reactions and nerve interactions rather than dealing with actual phenomenological experience of consciousness. For a further explanation, see Wallace, "Why the West," 12.

a co-developing package that gave us a reproductive advantage. The logical constructs that we have are useful on the scale at which we live and act.

It seems that perhaps our logical constructs are inappropriate to understand reality at the quantum level. As Richard Feynman, one of the leading theorist of quantum electrodynamics, said, "It is safe to say that nobody understands quantum mechanics." Perhaps we really cannot understand it. Perhaps reality at the quantum level does not follow the laws of logic that apply to our experience. Perhaps it is not natural to us. We have already discovered that objects in motion at close to the speed of light behave in ways that are counter-intuitive. If Pinker is right, perhaps we do not know this logic because we did not evolve an ability to understand it. We did not consciously operate at the quantum level on the savannas of Africa, so there was no evolutionary advantage to being able to reason about reality at that level. Now that we do operate at that level, the rules could seem strange because they actually are strange and we have not developed the ability to reason about them. It is more difficult to believe that Aquinas would allow that something in the universe operated with fundamentally different logic than that which governs the world as we experience it. Aquinas might have said that the world of quantum physics was very far away from our world of sensation, which makes it difficult to understand, but not fundamentally impossible to understand, as some interpretations of quantum physics have it. Although, if one allows that there might be different rules of logic in different areas of reality, the rules which govern quantum occurrences would not have needed to have been implanted in our nature because we have no need to know it in order to love and function in the world. God made us to find happiness and learn through experiencing the world at this macroscopic level, so there really is no need for God to have given us a particular ability to sense and understand things on the quantum level. It would be more likely, one might think, that God would have given us an ability to see immaterial reality and God directly, since knowing about these realities is more essential to our ultimate happiness, but God did not give us these abilities either. There are an infinite number of things that we could know that are unnecessary for our ultimate salvation. We enjoy learning them and knowing them, but the particulars of what we know in these areas are outside of God's plan. Since quantum physics developed in the Western world, Buddhism has not had as much chance to contemplate its strangeness. The Dalai Lama is currently in dialogue with scientists over these discoveries and is taking the stance of a learner, leaving himself free from evaluating its import at this time. However, since Tsongkhapa believed that logic applies only to the conventional level and breaks down on the ultimate level, it is not difficult to believe that he could have allowed that logic as we know it did not function on the conventional but quantum level.

Consciousness and Free Will

Consciousness and free will both seem on the surface to be quite straightforward concepts. Our consciousness is our awareness of the world around us and our thoughts within us, and our free will denotes our ability to make autonomous decisions as independent actors in the world. As we dig deeper, we find that these concepts are notoriously difficult to pin down, and more difficult yet to explain. Further complicating matters is that the different views of the human person make for different understandings of the salient features of consciousness and free will between our various authors, making it difficult to compare them in a straightforward manner. Each of these authors believes in the validity of consciousness and agrees that humans have free will, but they mean different things by these and hold them for different reasons.

Steven Pinker writes that consciousness and free will are subjective experiences that are ultimately a mystery, beyond our ability to understand.[12] Not that we simply have yet to understand it, but it might be impossible for us to understand because we have come upon a fundamental limit—the mind's ability to understand itself. There are three meanings one could have for consciousness: 1) "Being alive, awake, and aware"; 2) having access to short-term memories, rational thoughts, decision making, and the like; and 3) the first-person subjective experience we call sentience.[13] The first meaning is the common, imprecise use of the word that is difficult to pin down. The second one has a precise meaning that science is actively investigating. The most promising new scientific approach is seeing consciousness as a global workspace.[14] The brain has many processes for analyzing different types of data. These processes use different parts of the brain and run in parallel. In addition, the theory goes, the brain has developed a master

---

12. For his thoughts on consciousness see Pinker, *How the Mind Works*, 566. For free will see Pinker, *Blank Slate*, 424.

13. Pinker, *How the Mind Works*, 134–35.

14. Pinker, *How the Mind Works*, 137–43. For a more detailed explanation with an excellent summary of the supporting research see Dehaene, *Consciousness and the Brain*.

agent or executive process that runs on top and listens to these various subroutines, temporarily moving the results of whichever of these subroutines calls the loudest for attention into a global workspace that can be accessed simultaneously by many parts of the brain. This global workspace is the seat of awareness. The executive process has very limited processing bandwidth compared to the rest of the processing of ideas going on in our brains, but it has the ability to arbitrate between the various subprocesses, choosing one solution from among them and marking a problem solved so that the rest of the processors can move on to other work. The global workspace is what we experience as our moving consciousness. There are indications that it is housed in the frontal lobes of our brains.

While consciousness in the sense of access to data seems to be becoming understood, there is no consensus about what sentience might be.[15] Some scientists say that sentience is simply a quality of consciousness as access and is thus a mere subjective and definitional difference—a pseudo-problem. Pinker does not hold this position, and sees sentience as a fundamental datum of experience that cannot be explained away nor even addressed by his computational theory of mind. Sentience "floats in its own plane, high above the causal chains of psychology and neuroscience." Sentience is what defines the unity over time of an "I" beyond the series of brain states and bits of information we process. This is an important issue with ethical implications. "The concept of sentience underlies our certainty that torture is wrong and that disabling a robot is the destruction of property but disabling a person is murder. It is the reason that the death of a loved one does not impart to us just self-pity at our loss but the uncomprehending pain of knowing that the person's thoughts and pleasures have vanished forever."

Our experience of free will also seems so different from our normal concepts of causation that it seems "to belong in a separate, divine realm."[16] But in trying to use our minds to understand our minds, we cannot get outside of our brains to look back at them and check. This quandary is like the theories of quantum physics that defy our ability to understand them. This should be expected, however, since "if the mind is a biological organ rather than a window onto reality, there should be truths that are literally inconceivable, and limits to how well we can ever grasp the discoveries of science. . . . We have every reason to believe that consciousness

---

15. Pinker, *How the Mind Works*, 144–48.
16. Pinker, *Blank Slate*, 424.

and decision making arise from the electrochemical activity of neural networks in the brain. But how moving molecules should throw off subjective feelings (as opposed to mere intelligent computations) and how they bring about choices that we freely make (as opposed to behavior that is caused) remain deep enigmas to our Pleistocene psyches."[17]

A common scientific explanation that tries to make sense of this quandary is that consciousness is an emergent property of brains. An emergent property emerges when smaller components come together and was not present when they were apart, but does not require anything else to be present. For example, the properties of water, such as wetness, emerge when hydrogen and oxygen combine at a ratio of two to one. They are not present in hydrogen or oxygen alone. Some naturalists have posited that consciousness is an emergent property of the brain—experienced as quite different from the chemical reactions of the brain, though not caused by something other than these chemical reactions.[18] Many modern scientists see life as an emergent property of matter. As Pier Luigi Luisi explains, "The separate components of a living cell, such as DNA, proteins, sugars, and lipids, or even the cellular organelles, such as vesicles and mitochondria, are per se inanimate substances. From these non-living components, life emerges once a given space-time organization occurs, without the need to assume any transcendent or mysterious force."[19] These ideas can be extended to explain the conscious self as "an emergent property arising from the simultaneous juxtaposition of feelings, memory, thoughts, emotions." Just as water is made up of only hydrogen and oxygen in a particular relationship with no mysterious other substance added, even though it has properties that are quite different from both hydrogen and oxygen, the conscious self is made up of mental processes such as feelings, memory, thoughts, etc. in a particular juxtaposition. Consciousness has different properties than its component parts, but these properties emerge from their combination without the addition of any other special substance. Pinker believes that sentience just might be an emergent property of the brain, but to make this plausible, we would need to have a theory that could answer questions such as whether a computer simulating human cognition is conscious, or what it is like to be a bat.[20] We do not have such a theory and might never

17. Pinker, *Blank Slate*, 239–40.
18. Luisi, *Mind and Life*, 63–64.
19. Luisi, *Mind and Life*, 64.
20. Pinker, *How the Mind Works*, 145–46.

be able to create and test one because this would involve our brain trying to understand itself in totality.

Pinker's view of free will as mystery is not without content. Though ultimate understanding eludes us, we do know some things about ourselves. Embedded in this view is that free will is something humans have and computers do not. If free will simply meant the ability to choose preferences based on available data using an internal criteria (the autonomous part), computers could be programmed with sufficient complexity to qualify. Even as we learn more about the causes of our behavior, how our brains process data and make decisions, we still find no deterministic connection between inputs and actual choices made by people. This preserves the need to affirm personal responsibility in decision making.[21] Pinker also wants to rule out Rene Descartes's idea that our mind, with its consciousness and free will, is of a different substance than our bodies and inhabits them, as Gilbert Ryle derisively labeled it, as a ghost in the machine.[22] In Descartes's model, the mind (the ghost) is free because it makes its choices apart from the machinery of the brain. Pinker believes that this view is wrong because our mental decisions are obviously made with our brain, which has evolved numerous mental processes that condition the way we make choices in predictable ways.[23] But conditioning our decisions is not the same thing as completely determining them. The ghost in the machine view would also be a dangerous idea to embrace because it would erode society's ability to modify people's behavior. Pinker cites a thought experiment of the philosopher Daniel Dennett, that if people had an utterly free will as in the ghost in the machine, morality and law would be pointless.[24] A completely free will could not be controlled by fear of punishment or the twinge of guilt. Being free from material constraints, it could simply choose to ignore these things in the future. Experiments show, however, that the will is predictably, if only probabilistically, affected by the prospect of esteem and shame.

Tsongkhapa's Buddhist position on free will also emphasizes personal responsibility.[25] The inviolate laws of karma detail how freely chosen actions in this life have specific consequences in future rebirths. As we have seen earlier, the karmic effects of any action are more affected by the motivation

---

21. Pinker, *Blank Slate*, 185.
22. Pinker, *Blank Slate*, 8–9.
23. Pinker, *Blank Slate*, 166–67.
24. Pinker, *Blank Slate*, 176.
25. See the section on Ethics in ch. 2, pp. 34–39.

behind the action than the mechanics of it. For instance, the karmic effects of murdering someone do not depend on whether one commits the offense oneself or hires it out, but they are very much affected by doing it out of malice or wanting to create suffering in the victim.[26] A murder carried out because of compassion, as when it would save a bad person from generating a great amount of negative karma by killing them before they committed a series of heinous crimes, could even be considered virtuous, even though it might result in one lifetime being reborn in hell.[27] All of this is premised on the fact that individual mind-streams are free to make choices and are karmically responsible for the choices they make. When a buddha works to help another individual escape the chains of ignorance binding them to samsara, the buddha does not change the laws of karma or directly affect the person's karma in any way. Rather, the buddha can see the different karmic effects of various actions that are available to the individual at that point, and then can help the individual to make the right choices to bring the best karmic strands to fruition and to avoid the bad karmic strands.[28] The individual has to make the choices. The buddha or bodhisattva can only inform.

Having a free will does not imply that there is an essentially existing self. There is not. Nothing exists essentially. Everything comes about through causes and conditions in dependence upon other things. Nothing happens of necessity or is essentially self-caused. But there is a functioning self, a dependently existing illusion we call a mind-stream, and it has a will and can make choices. At any point, our will is conditioned by many things—our ignorance or wisdom, the effects of past karmic actions, the lure of sensual desires—but our will is never so conditioned that it is fully constrained in its choice. As we gain wisdom and learn to see the consequences of our actions, we are able to make better choices. As we overcome our momentary, sensual desires that rage on the surface so that we can see through them to our deeper desire to free ourselves and all sentient beings from the cycle of suffering that is samsara, we become more free to make better choices. A buddha can appear within our mind-stream to help guide

---

26. See pp. 35–36.

27. Harvey, *Introduction*, 136–37.

28. For an explanation of how the Buddha explicitly sees the dependently arising karmic streams of other sentient beings, see Hopkins, *Tsongkhapa's Final Exposition*, 348–54. For a short description of how the Buddha acts on behalf of others, see Gyamtso, *Buddha Nature*, 385–86.

our choices, but our dependently existing self has to make the right choices in order to move forward.

Consciousness is just as difficult to pin down. As the Dalai Lama explains, "Even in Buddhism there is an implicit recognition of the difficulty of identifying what consciousness is. Although we are aware that consciousness exists, when we try to define it, it becomes very nebulous and difficult to pinpoint. But in principle, Buddhism maintains that it is possible to recognize experientially what consciousness is and identify it."[29] Words cannot describe consciousness itself because words describe the things that we are conscious of. Words typically used to denote consciousness are "clarity" and "luminosity," but these are not thought to define it. Great meditators can experience the most subtle forms of consciousness, but their experiences cannot be conveyed to others through words. It is an experience one must have for oneself.

The Dalai Lama holds that consciousness, however difficult it might be to define, is not an emergent property of matter. While it is true that embodied consciousnesses such as the human visual perception rely on sense organs and the brain and cannot exist without them, consciousness itself, the luminous aspect of these mental processes, cannot emerge from matter.[30] Consciousness is beginningless. It existed before this universe existed, before the Big Bang created matter and energy. When matter became sufficiently organized to support it, consciousness entered our material realm through sentient beings. The physical properties of matter—brains and so forth—affect the gross manifestations of consciousness, but they do not give rise to consciousness. As the Dalai Lama explains, "According to Buddhist principles, consciousness can arise only from a continuum of phenomena similar to itself, in the same way that formations of mass-energy give rise to formations of mass-energy. It is a similar continuum. Subtle consciousness is a radically different type of phenomenon; therefore it can arise only from phenomena similar to itself. Matter, configurations of mass-energy, is radically dissimilar to consciousness. Therefore, only a stream of consciousness can give rise to a later stream of consciousness. Matter cannot transform into or become consciousness."[31] Alan Wallace adds, "The Buddhist theory is that our subjective awareness is not brain-based awareness, but rather brain-conditioned awareness. Human

---

29. Luisi, *Mind and Life*, 160.
30. Luisi, *Mind and Life*, 157.
31. Luisi, *Mind and Life*, 161.

consciousness is indeed an emergent property, but it emerges from a deeper level of consciousness, one that carries on from lifetime to lifetime, and is then conditioned by the brain."[32] For Buddhists, consciousness existed long before this physical universe existed. Buddhism has a notion of many kalpas, or long eons of time in which a particular world comes to be and passes away, so it could dialogue with modern science about the relative beginning of human consciousness on the planet Earth, but it has a much broader view of consciousness as a whole.

Thomas Aquinas doesn't have a concept that directly corresponds to our idea of consciousness, and instead talks about things like understanding or conceiving or imagining. Modern Thomists will often accept an idea of consciousness as the unity of our sensual and intellectual interpretations of reality. Following what Aquinas says about the cognitive life, modern Thomists, like modern Buddhists, think of consciousness as brain-conditioned but not brain-based. Consciousness is based in the whole person, which has material and immaterial capacities. For Aquinas, understanding is a capacity that grasps the natures of material things. If it were constrained by materiality, with its own material nature, understanding would be distorted, as hearing would be impaired if our ears made a noise.[33]

Although Aquinas doesn't think we can look inside ourselves in the way some modern philosophers do, he does think we can, as it were, look over our own shoulders while we are thinking, and so be aware of our own understanding.[34] Our understanding comes from our experience of the world, and as we understand we also experience our own understanding.[35] This is the nature of mind, and it happens automatically. We can also subsequently reflect on the nature of our minds and come to know our consciousness in a different, universal way. This gives us a deeper understanding of our consciousness, but it takes careful and subtle inquiry, the kind made by philosophers, and is not done by everyone.

Our understanding is immaterial and is done by our intellect, but this is a power of the whole person. The whole human being understands, and not simply one part of us.[36] Our intellect must be united to our bodies because the same person understands that he knows and that he senses the

---

32. Luisi, *Mind and Life*, 167.
33. Aquinas, *Summa Theologiae*, 1:75.2.
34. Aquinas, *Summa Theologiae*, 1:76.1.
35. Aquinas, *Summa Theologiae*, 1:87.1.
36. Aquinas, *Summa Theologiae*, 1:76.1.

world. Sensing the world requires a body, so our intellect must be somehow united to our bodies. It is absurd to think of our intellect as a motor that drives our bodies (the ghost in the machine) because that presupposes too neat a division. It's not as if we are a physical thing moved from outside, understanding because we have an intellectual motor, as it were. We do not understand because we are moved by our intellect; rather, we are moved by our intellect because we understand the world as in some way good, and so desire it. Understanding belongs to us, and if it were attributed to an intellectual form that was not united to our bodies, it would be attributed to something other than us. In this case, it would not be we who understood the world, but these separated substances.[37]

Aquinas links the freedom of the will, personal responsibility, and our knowledge of the world, as do our other thinkers.[38] According to Aquinas, our intellect moves us through our appetites. These can be sense appetites, as when we smell delicious food and want to eat it, much like another animal would. In addition, if we understand something to be good, our will desires it. This relies on innate tendency to incline to the good and on our knowledge of the world around us. We can only desire something that we know, and we can only desire it insofar as we perceive it to be good. Our will is free in ways our body is not, because we're able to understand the world in many incompatible ways, and so we can choose, to a great extent, what seems to us good. Our will cannot be externally coerced the way our body can. While the actions of our body may be constrained from without—someone could physically pick us up and carry us to where we do not want to go, or move our arm against our will—our will cannot be compelled by any external force to choose against what it perceives to be the good. Things such as fear make it harder to exercise our freedom, but cannot take our freedom away entirely.

In this life, everything that we perceive is good in some ways and not in others. Only God is goodness itself, and God is not a thing in this world—God transcends the world. So nothing in this world can make us will it. We can come to desire something by considering the ways in which it is good, and we can come to not desire it by focusing on the ways in which it is bad. Our wills are not constrained to set themselves on any particular good that

---

37. In the same article Aquinas gives other reasons why it is absurd to think of the intellect as a motor driving our bodies. These are sufficient to make the point here, but the others are an interesting insight into just how differently Aquinas and Rene Descartes view the human person.

38. For Aquinas on the will, see Aquinas, *Summa Theologiae*, 1:79–83.

we perceive, so we are responsible for what our wills set themselves on. We always have to weigh competing goods based on our own understanding and the relative weights we set between various goods. Our will follows our understanding and can serve us better as our understanding grows, so we are also responsible to inform ourselves with sufficient knowledge to be able to exercise our wills well.

In a line very much like Pinker, Aquinas writes, "Man is free to make decisions. Otherwise counsels, precepts, prohibitions, rewards and punishment would all be pointless."[39] Inanimate objects and plants do not have free wills. You cannot successfully exhort a rock or a tree to move. With training you can command some animals to act in particular ways, but Aquinas holds that animals do not have free will because they do not rely on the sophisticated level of understanding of general principles that stands behind our wills. A dog can be trained not to eat meat left on a counter, but it cannot come to understand the pros and cons of eating meat and so become an ethical vegetarian. Computers and robots do not have free wills because they lack the unity that a soul provides, but they could be programmed to simulate the functioning of a free will.[40] Pinker was looking for a theory that would explain why killing a person was murder while destroying a robot was destruction of property. Aquinas offers this, that the robot lacks a unity to make it a single thing. Disassembling a robot is not morally troubling, because it was assembled in the first place. It is not naturally one thing, and consequently not alive. But would this satisfy Pinker?

Pinker's critique of the ghost in the machine does not weigh against Aquinas's position. For Aquinas, the soul and body form a unity; the soul does not inhabit the body like a ghost in a machine. The will belongs to the soul, so it is affected by the body. If our brain is impaired so that we cannot think clearly, our will will be affected. We all find we are liable to be more irritable and impatient when we are hot, for example. The ghost in the machine critique would also not fit Tsongkhapa, since he believes that there is no soul at all. The heart of this critique asserted that people could not be controlled by society or held responsible for their choices if their wills were entirely unaffected by what happened in the physical world to their body.

---

39. Aquinas, *Summa Theologiae*, 1:83.1.

40. This is different than arguing that robots do not have free will because they do not understand the world *in some sense*. A parallel argument could be made from a Thomistic perspective that robots do not understand because they lack the unity this term implies. Their memories might remember, and their CPUs might process the information, but they lack a unity to point to one thing that understands.

But both Tsongkhapa and Aquinas seek to empower people to look beyond the narrow concerns of what is best for themselves in their individual lives and to be motivated by deeper truths that transcend their personal welfare, recognizing that the greatest goal is not personal security but universal redemption. Thus, both Buddhism and Christianity are replete with stories of heroic people who endured pain and struggle and imprisonment for the sake of truth and justice. Think of Joan of Arc, who defied social conventions and established authority to support the King of France, eventually paying with her life by being burned at the stake after a politically motivated trial. She believed she had been told by visions of angels and saints to join in the fight for her country against the English. In an age dominated by men, she was a powerful and effective military leader, leading the French army to victory in the siege of Orléans, before being captured by the English and tried for heresy, though she was later exonerated by a papal court, and finally declared a saint. There is also the story of Namo Buddha, Siddhartha Gautama in a previous life, who went on a hunting expedition and came upon a wounded tigress who was too weak to even nurse her cubs.[41] Moved with compassion, but unwilling to kill another creature to save this one, the Buddha cut himself and fed the tigress his own blood until she had the strength to get up and kill and eat him. Are the stories of Joan of Arc and Namo Buddha examples of heroism to be emulated or of disruptive forces in society that need to be suppressed? Just how free do we want people's wills to be? Rather than basing societal order on a system of rewards and punishments that tap into our primal needs, would we be better off to base it on the idea of motivating people to become bodhisattvas or saints that speak to our greatest hopes?

Arguments For and Against Creation

Where did this the universe come from? How did we get here? Why is there something rather than nothing? These are essential questions that shape and are shaped by a world-picture. The answers to these questions are quite different for Aquinas, Tsongkhapa, and Pinker.

Aquinas pictures an all-powerful, loving God intentionally creating the world in order to share his overflowing love and joy. In his *Summa Theologiae*, Aquinas gives five famous proofs for the existence of God, which can be turned around and become five proofs for why the world

---

41. Namo Buddha Monastery, "Ancient Story."

cannot be its own explanation and thus stands in need of a creator.[42] From the point of view of creation, perhaps Aquinas's third way most easily helps us see why the universe is dependent upon God.[43] The things we see around us are contingent—they come into existence through other things that already exist, and then they go out of existence. If everything were contingent like this, then there could have been a time when nothing existed. If this were so, then nothing would exist now because nothing could have come into existence. This is clearly not the case, so there must be something that exists in its own right, something that has self-existence and always exists, which could be the basis for the existence of things that are contingent. This is existence itself (*ipsum esse subsistens*), which is God.

Aquinas offered a similar proof that reinforces the "third way" in a pamphlet *On the Eternity of the World*. This proof, however, is also open to the world not having a beginning in time.[44] Aquinas believed that the world was created with a beginning in time because the book of Genesis relates the story of its creation, but this is a matter of religious faith and revelation rather than a necessity of reason.[45] Rather than being about a flick of an on-switch at the beginning of time, Aquinas reasoned that creation was about the dependence of the universe at every moment on God's existence. The things of this world are contingent, they come into being and pass away. Their existence is thus not part of their nature, it comes from outside of them. What comes from within something is prior to it in its nature than that which comes from without, so in the nature

---

42. Aquinas, *Summa Theologiae*, 1:2.3.

43. The full text of Aquinas's third way: "The third way is based on what need not be and on what must be, and runs as follows. Some of the things we come across can be but need not be, for we find them springing up and dying away, thus sometimes in being and sometimes not. Now everything cannot be like this, for a thing that need not be, once was not; and if everything need not be, once upon a time there was nothing. But if that were true there would be nothing even now, because something that does not exist can only be brought into being by something already existing. So that if nothing was in being nothing could be brought into being, and nothing would be in being now, which contradicts observation. Not everything therefore is the sort of thing that need not be; there has got to be something that must be. Now a thing that must be, may or may not owe this necessity to something else. But just as we must stop somewhere in a series of causes, so also in the series of things which must be and owe this to other things. One is forced therefore to suppose something which must be, and owes this to no other thing than itself; indeed it itself is the cause that other things must be."

44. The same argument is made more briefly at Aquinas, *Summa Theologiae*, 1:46.2.

45. Perhaps Aquinas also holds this because the Fourth Lateran Council speaks of creation as having a beginning (*ab initio temporis*).

of contingent things, non-being is prior to being. It is the nature of each contingent being, such as everything that we observe in the world, that it has the potential to exist but, if left to itself, it would not exist. This is true whether or not the thing has always existed in time, because we are speaking of an order of nature and not an order of time. If every thing has the nature of non-being over being, no thing would exist. Thus, there must be something whose nature is to exist which gives its being to things whose priority is not to exist. This we call God, or being-itself. The reception of being by contingent things is not done in time, as if the thing had to not exist temporally prior to its coming into existence. The reception of being happens instantaneously. Contingent things exist because they receive existence from existence-itself, as the daylight lasts while the sun shines. Even if the world was not created finite in time but went backwards in history forever, it would still be dependent upon God.

Modern Thomists do not usually interpret the creation stories literally, so they would be free to entertain the idea of creation reaching backward in time with no beginning, but there is no great movement in this direction. Modern Thomists usually have a knowledge of modern science, and the prevalence of the Big Bang theory of creation makes most moderns comfortable with picturing a beginning of space-time. What modern Thomists are not free to believe is that space-time exists independently of God.

Steven Pinker does not get heavily involved in philosophies of the creation of the universe. He is not a physicist. As a psychologist and neurologist he is quite critical of the role religions have played throughout history in sanctioning violence, and he has shown how we do not need to resort to the idea of god to ground morality, explain the human mind, or find meaning in life. He considers himself to be an atheist, and like most scientists, accepts the reigning explanation of physicists that the universe was created about fourteen billion years ago in the Big Bang.

For this section, then, we will turn to other scientists who have taken on the scientific question of why there is something rather than nothing. Ideas are broadly shared in this area, and there are several places we could turn for good explanations of consensus opinions. To represent the field we will present two related arguments, one from Stephen Hawking and the other from Lawrence Krauss with the support of Richard Dawkins.

Physicist Stephen Hawking has proposed a theory of how we can think about the Big Bang without needing a divine figure to start it out because although it has a beginning in time, the universe does not have a moment of creation.[46] The laws of physics can explain how the universe develops over time. If we knew the initial conditions of the universe we could use the laws of physics to predict the unfolding of the universe over its entire course of history. These laws seem to be finely tuned to create intelligent life like ourselves. If any of the basic constants of the universe were only slightly different, we would not exist. Since each of the constants of the universe seem as if they could be different, it seems highly improbable that they all just happened to line up perfectly to create exactly this perfect universe. Such fine-tuning could be explained by the hand of a creator who intentionally crafted the laws in order to bring about intelligent life. Another explanation is that there are an almost infinite number of universes or regions within this universe that each have slightly different values for these constants and we are in the one (or part) that has parameters just right for intelligent beings like us to develop. This is known as the anthropic principle. It has some problems of its own, but when combined with another new idea, the inflationary principle, it can make the initial conditions required to create intelligent beings such as ourselves broad enough to be plausibly possible.

There is, however, another problem. The Big Bang is theorized to begin at a point with infinite density. All of the macroscopic laws that govern the universe, such as gravity, break down at this singularity. So while God might know the initial conditions of the universe, we could never work them out, so we are precluded from understanding the universe through applying these laws. Fortunately, we have begun to understand quantum physics, which gives us laws that work over minute spaces that existed at the Big Bang. While we have not worked out all of the details of quantum gravity, we know that over the distances that applied at the start of the Big Bang, time ceases to become distinguishable from distance and we end up with a Euclidean four-dimensional world, opening up new possibilities. A world that obeyed Euclidian geometry would not have singularities at zero distance. Using quantum gravity we could posit a space-time that had no edges or boundary conditions and would explain the Big Bang.

A no-boundary condition world would be like a globe, having no edges. One could keep moving in a straight line forever without getting to the end, yet it is still a finite size because you end up going in circles. It would be like heading south on our planet Earth. One could move south only for so long before reaching the south pole, at which point every

---

46. Hawking, *Brief History of Time*, chap. 8. The following explanation is taken from this chapter.

direction would be north. One could not travel further south than the south pole, and this is not a mystery. The south pole is simply a reference point. It is not the beginning of the world. Passing through it does not affect your travel, just the description of your travel. In the same way, the Euclidian space-time that describes the universe might be such that you cannot go back further in time than a particular point without needing to posit that point as a beginning.

The reason why this would be an appealing configuration is because

> there would be no boundary to space-time and so there would be no need to specify the behavior at the boundary. There would be no singularities at which the laws of science broke down, and no edge of space-time at which one would have to appeal to God or some new law to set the boundary conditions for space-time. One could say: "The boundary condition of the universe is that it has no boundary." The universe would be completely self-contained and not affected by anything outside itself. It would neither be created nor destroyed, It would just BE.[47]

A universe such as this would have no need of creation or of a transcendent God, and could, in theory, be completely known by the intelligent creatures within it.

The no-boundary condition is just a proposal. To know if such a mathematical description fit the universe, we would have create quantum descriptions of the entire universe, everything in it, and sum up the probabilities of its various histories over time and see if they matched what we see in the universe. This is impossible for two reasons. First, such equations are difficult to create even for small systems, so they would be impossible to create for the entire universe. Second, we only have one universe to use for our data. We cannot run multiple versions of the universe and see how they compare with our model. Taking these two problems into account, we can at least run some calculations on a highly simplified model universe and see if the way our universe is unfolding is at least possible and perhaps probable. One case that has been tried predicts that under no-boundary conditions, despite the quantum fluctuations present at the Big Bang, the universe would expand equally in all directions on a macroscopic scale. This is in line with what we see. This test could have shown the no-boundary condition to be false, and it did not, so that is at least a first glimmer of confirmation.

---

47. Hawking, *Brief History of Time*, 141.

Lawrence Krauss shares Stephen Hawking's views of physics and has proposed another way that the laws of physics remove the need for recourse to God as an explanatory principle for the universe. Rather than a no-boundary condition for the universe, Krauss argues that, just given the laws of physics, the Big Bang that created this particular universe was bound to happen. He lays his arguments out in his aptly titled book, *A Universe from Nothing: Why There Is Something Rather than Nothing*.

Krauss notes that arguments from creation are a last refuge of those who want to justify their belief in God:

> The central problem with the notion of creation is that it appears to require some externality, something outside of the system itself, to preexist, in order to create the conditions necessary for the system to come into being. This is usually where the notion of God—some external agency existing separate from space, time, and indeed from physical reality itself—comes in, because the buck seems to be required to stop somewhere. But in this sense God seems to me to be a rather facile semantic solution to the deep question of creation. I think this is best explained within the context of a slightly different example: the origin of morality, which I first learned from my friend Steven Pinker.[48]

Just as Pinker explained how our sense of morality arose through evolution without recourse to a divine lawgiver, Krauss elaborates how the universe could have come into existence without recourse to God as its creator. Krauss's analysis is based on some remarkable, non-intuitive discoveries in modern physics, which have been largely confirmed through statistical verification. The most striking one is that empty space weighs something, apart from any matter or energy that might be present in it.[49] Quantum theory predicts that in the absence of matter, empty space itself will spontaneously produce particle-antiparticle pairs.[50] These theories can be extended to deal with gravity as well, and "a quantum theory of gravity allows for the creation, albeit perhaps momentarily, of space itself."[51] In order for the universe that we see to have spontaneously come into existence and grown to the size that we see, the basic constants that are embedded in the physical laws of the universe would have to be quite finely tuned. One could believe

---

48. Krauss, *Universe from Nothing*, 171.
49. Krauss, *Universe from Nothing*, chap. 4.
50. Krauss, *Universe from Nothing*, chap. 6.
51. Krauss, *Universe from Nothing*, 163.

that some deity sat and turned all the knobs just so in order to create us, or one could invoke the anthropic principle and multiverses or string theory to argue that all variations of these laws could exist simultaneously, and we are in this one because this one supports life like us.[52]

The significance of this argument is that we do not need anything outside the universe to explain the universe. As Richard Dawkins explains in the afterword of the book, "Not only does physics tell us how something could have come from nothing, it goes further, by Krauss's account, and shows us that nothingness is unstable: something was almost bound to spring into existence from it."[53] Krauss has kept to his promise of explaining how something outside the system did not have to preexist in order to get something from nothing, but the system itself has to preexist, so an argument could be made that he has shifted the goalposts but not resolved the fundamental quandary.

Moving now to Mahayana Buddhism, we begin by noting that beginningless nescience is a foundational principle for Tsongkhapa. We have been suffering through an endless cycle of rebirths in samsara through beginningless time because of our ignorance. If we ever hope to escape, we first need to recognize and detest this reality. Our mind-streams are beginningless; they have no creation and no creator. While consciousness is beginningless, the material world is not. We have seen above how the Dalai Lama holds that consciousness could not be an emergent property of matter because it has existed forever, but there is more to the Dalai Lama's reasoning and it connects directly to the current topic:

> Buddhist philosophy employs the logical reasoning that if consciousness can arise from matter, then we have to posit a beginning to consciousness and a beginning to the continuum of sentient beings. By extension of that reasoning, we would also have to accept a beginning to the whole universe, which opens up a whole can of worms. Since Buddhism rejects that and accepts the beginningless continuum of consciousness, therefore it also accepts the beginningless continuum of sentient beings. Because sentient beings have no beginning, Buddhism interprets the evolution of the physical universe as intimately interdependent with the sentient beings who inhabit and experience the external world.
>
> As to the question of why it matters, first, it presents a philosophical problem. If we are forced to accept a beginning to the

---

52. Krauss, *Universe from Nothing*, chap. 8.
53. Krauss, *Universe from Nothing*, 189.

universe, we have two options. Either something comes from nothing, or we have to posit a divine creator, a transcendent being, neither of which Buddhism finds comfortable. Second, from a soteriological point of view, a single lifetime is an extremely brief duration in which to achieve liberation and enlightenment. It's said to be possible in principle to achieve enlightenment in three years, three months, and three days, but this is much like Communist propaganda. The chances of it happening are so remote you might as well forget about it! Even in a lifetime of sixty years, the chances of achieving enlightenment for most of us are remote. So we need a bit more time.[54]

This short passage highlights many differences between Buddhists, Christians, and naturalists. Buddhists believe that the sentient beings living now are manifestations of mind-streams that existed before the creation of the universe. Consciousness transcends not simply lives, but eons, kalpas, and universes. Modern naturalists have worked hard to understand how sentience arises within the material universe with the presumption that intelligence and sentience began with *Homo sapiens* or our not-so-distant relatives and emerges within each new fetus when its central nervous system becomes sufficiently developed. Christians believe that sentience begins anew in each human soul as it is created directly by God and united to the fetus (or blastocyst; it is unclear when this happens and probably impossible to know).

Gelukpa Buddhists and Thomist Christians both believe, against naturalists, that the consciousness that exists in individual humans is not created by matter but stems from consciousness that existed before the beginning of the universe—in Buddhism, from beginningless individual mind-streams entering into material existence; in Christianity, created individually and united to matter by God, who is also without beginning. Naturalists believe that consciousness arises from matter and perhaps can best be thought of as an epiphenomenon of matter that has reached a particular level of organization. Buddhists and Christians hold that consciousness is composed from something utterly different than matter.

These differences about the nature of the human person lead to different views of creation. The Dalai Lama is undoubtedly aware of Aquinas's proofs for the existence of God, and cannot countenance getting something from nothing nor a pre-existent creator. Krauss's proof that a creator is not necessary because the laws of nature demand spontaneous creation from a vacuum

54. Luisi, *Mind and Life*, 163–64.

do not overcome this objection, because the laws of nature are not nothing. In Krauss's argument, the laws of nature exist and are the cause of matter. They beg the further question, where did the laws come from? How do they exist? Aquinas's alternative, which the Dalai Lama references, is a self-existing transcendent being that creates the universe, something which neither Buddhists nor naturalists allow. Krauss believes that one could believe in this creator God or a much simpler explanation—that the laws themselves simply exist. Invoking Occam's razor that we should not unnecessarily complicate explanations, Krauss prefers the latter.[55] But rather than the simpler solution, it seems to simply leave the question unanswered.

The Buddhist solution posits an infinite regression in time so that there is no creation. This is similar to Stephen Hawking's solution in that Hawking's circular time vector needs no starting point, although Hawking's solution also allows for the universe to have existed for a finite amount of time. The Buddhist view also allows for this particular universe to have existed a finite amount of time, even though consciousness has no beginning. Aquinas reasoned that even if the universe would have existed forever, it is filled with contingent things that could possibly not exist if left to themselves. If everything existed contingently, then nothing would exist, so the presence of contingent things requires there to be something that exists in its own right, undergirding contingent existence at every moment. Aquinas's reasoning is known by many Buddhists and naturalists, but they are not convinced by it.[56] Part of the reason might be that Aquinas's view equates God and being-itself and believes this to be obvious. It is obvious in Aquinas's picture of the world, since God as being-itself is a central part of the picture, but Buddhists and naturalists do not believe it to be true, and naturalists regularly ridicule it as conveniently imprecise. The Dalai Lama's argument relies on the truth of a particular fundamental feature of his world-picture, beginningless nescience, so it is not convincing to others who do not already share this

---

55. Krauss, *Universe from Nothing*, 146.

56. However, there is a minority view within Tibetan Buddhism that makes exactly this argument, arguing for the existence of the tathagatagarbha complete with its qualities at an ultimate level in a different mode of existence to explain how anything exists at the mundane level. A main expositor of this position, Dolpopa, writes, "Without support there can be nothing supported, and so forth, which leads to the extreme consequence that without an absolute there would be no relative" (Stearns, *Dolpopa*, 146). For a discussion of the differences between Dolpopa and Tsongkhapa on this, see Hopkins, *Final Exposition of Wisdom*, 271–317.

picture. Hawking's argument gets around a problem that was created in one scientific description of the issue by offering a different description of the issue that does not suffer from the same problem. But rather than addressing the questions of why there is something rather than nothing and how you can get something from nothing, the no-boundary Euclidian space-time model simply obscures these issues. They are not features that show up in the model and so the question is not addressed.

The soteriological question of salvation and/or attaining ultimate goals is also seen quite differently in these various traditions. Buddhists believe that we have each spent countless lifetimes in nescience, building up bad karma and muddled beliefs. Few can undo so much damage in one lifetime.[57] Knowing that whatever headway we achieve in this life will also follow us into the next can motivate people to try to move forward. This logic is convincing for Buddhists. In contrast, Christians believe that no matter how hard we try, it is impossible to become perfect through our own effort, which is reflected in the Catholic doctrine of original sin. Fortunately, we do not have to become perfect in order to be saved. Salvation is a gift freely given by God, won for us by Christ, the God-man. In the end, God perfects us if we want God to do that, and we do not have to wait around for multiple lives to have that happen. In contrast yet again, Pinker and many naturalists believe that we only have this one life to do anything with. There is no other. We are free to set our own goals and to ascribe our own meaning to life and then work toward our goals. Any recourse to other lives or rewards in heaven simply distracts us from our task of making the most of this life. There is no master plan, no grand narrative of the universe, so it is up to us to make of this life what we want.

Each of these soteriological goals can be pursued in an individualistic or a communal way. In Pinker's view, there is no plan for the universe or for human nature.[58] This could lead people to simply grab all they could for themselves. But this is tempered by our evolution-driven nature as communal, social beings. Thus, many people find their greatest happiness in making the world a better place for others and for future generations. This is one of the reasons why we can be hopeful that the current global historical trend toward nonviolence will continue. Christians could simply worry about their own salvation, but a Catholic understanding of salva-

---

57. For more on the depth of our conditioning see Tsongkhapa, *Great Treatise*, 1:124–28.

58. Pinker, *How the Mind Works*, 165.

tion is that we are all in this together and work together for the salvation of all. Tsongkhapa's Mahayana critique of Theravadan Buddhism is that it is too individualistic. That is why the ideal practitioner is seen not as the arhat meditating in a cave, but a bodhisattva who consciously works for the salvation of all sentient beings. So all three of these views of salvation, while very different from each other, share the feature of being concerned with global well-being rather than individual salvation.

Finally, the "why"—is there a meaning in creation itself? Aquinas directly addresses this question and it is central to his picture of the world. The universe exists in order to share in God's love. Creation is an outpouring of God's superabundant love. God creates in order that creation itself can share in his joy and love. Buddhists believe that samsara exists because of beginningless nescience. Nescience was not created and it has no deeper meaning. It just is, and it leads necessarily to suffering. But recognizing this to be the case offers one the chance at having a meaningful life by reducing one's own and others' suffering. Naturalists who rely on science as the source of truth do not ascribe any meaning to the existence of the universe or any law or feature of the universe. They tend to resist any attribution to do so as an unjustified projection of our desire to ascribe meaning to the things and events of our world. Neither Krauss's nor Hawking's accounts of the creation of the universe ascribe any meaning to its existence, and part of the anthropic principle and the possibilities of multiple universes is to explain why we do not have to ascribe a meaning to our existence. The universe seems so finely tuned to intelligent life not by intention, but because we are looking at one universe out of a potentially infinite number that happened to have formed intelligent life. As Krauss points out, science does not give us "why" because that implicitly assumes a purpose.[59] Rather, science concentrates on how things happen. Krauss therefore takes the question to be "how is there something rather than nothing." This is indeed an interesting question, one that even Krauss admits we will probably never fully understand,[60] but it is not the same question as why it exists. This disconnect is perhaps what allows Krauss to assert theology's "intellectual bankruptcy" for vaguely defining "nothing" as "non-being" and having no explanation as to "how" the universe evolved.[61] Aquinas is quite precise in

---

59. Krauss, *Universe from Nothing*, 143.
60. Krauss, *Universe from Nothing*, 147.
61. Krauss, *Universe from Nothing*, preface.

his analysis of being and causality, and is much more concerned with why things happen than with how they do.

The Basis of Morality

Let us move on to a fundamentally different question: what are the guidelines to help us live a good life? This is the question of morality. Or course, what constitutes a good or a bad life is part of a fundamental picture of the world, and each of our thinkers has a different view on the subject, but each also has a way to ground their morality so that moral reasoning is not circular or arbitrary.

Thomas Aquinas believes that God has a plan for the world that includes human flourishing, so humans will flourish if they act in accord with this plan and will suffer as they depart from it. This is the basis of morality. God's plan is complex, well beyond our ability to comprehend, but we can learn enough about it to guide our lives by studying the world and listening to God's revelation. Through studying the world and reasoning about it we can come to understand the natural law, the way the world was meant to function. We also have a natural affinity for truth and goodness. As we learn more about the world we can make better decisions about how to act in ways that benefit ourselves, others, and the world that sustains us. Because it is sometimes difficult to know what is best and there can be errors in our knowledge, God has also given us revelation to help guide our decisions and to point us in the right direction. Since our reasoning ability, the natural law, and revelation all come from God, they can never be fundamentally opposed to each other. Our conscience, when rightly informed, can never be in disagreement with God's revelation.

Our flourishing here in this life is meant to ultimately give way to flourishing in the next life. Humans have an unlimited ability to know and to love, so our desire for the good in this life can never be completely satisfied. God has thus created a place for us in heaven where we can metaphorically see God face to face and be completely satisfied. There is a natural connection between our flourishing in this life and in heaven, but sometimes we are better off to forgo goods of this world in order to attain even greater goods in heaven.

Tsongkhapa also believes in a connection between living rightly here and attaining ultimate bliss after this life. Rather than the natural law, our actions should be guided by an awareness of the suffering that they cause and a knowledge of the laws of karma that govern our rebirths and the joys and tribulations we receive in any life.[62] These are not two separate fields. The suffering we cause and experience here is directly connected to the laws of karma that govern the universe. By coming to understand that our current situation is not the product of chance, but is the result of causes and conditions, choices we have made and actions we have taken in the past, we can come to make better decisions so that we can improve our future. We have made ourselves who we are through our own decisions and we are born into the right situation to fit who we are. The laws of karma are difficult though not impossible to discern, so we can rely on guidance from holy writings and from experts who can see them more clearly than we can. We do not simply need to take this on faith. We need teachers to guide us, but they only show us where to look and help us to see more clearly. Ultimately, we see for ourselves that Buddhist teachings are true, they fit and explain our deepest experiences of the world. To live rightly, then, is to live in such a way that we can attain ultimate bliss once we are freed from this current life.

Finding peace in this life is typically an essential part of this process, but there can be times when the best way for us to learn is through having experiences that seem to be the opposite of peaceful. Because each of us is different, we each have different consequences from actions that on the surface are equivalent. Something that might be good for one person, such as practicing a particular tantric practice, could have very bad consequences for another person. This is why it is important to work with a teacher whom one trusts. We can also enhance the karmic repercussions of our actions through attaching them to vows. For example, making a vow to perform a particular meditation every day would create more benefit every time we meditated, but we would also incur repercussions should we neglect this duty.

Christianity has a notion of vows as well, but this is a case of committing yourself to more than you are naturally required to do, not unlike a promise made to another human being. Morality for someone in vows is not fundamentally different than morality for someone without. We should keep our promises, whether to God or to others. And our other commitments remain more or less the same, even if circumstances might give one different rights or obligations. For example, those who have children have

---

62. For an explanation of how karma governs our life, see chapter 2, or Tsongkhapa, *Great Treatise*, chs. 13–14.

obligations to those children that others do not. In all of this, God gives aid to help us do what is right, and there might be special graces to enable those who have made vows to fulfill them, just as Christians believe that God gives grace to parents to help them be better parents.

Steven Pinker grounds morality in human flourishing, but in ways that can be measured and openly debated. He has proposed ten metrics we might consider to measure flourishing: lifespan, health, prosperity, peace, safety, openness of societies, education levels, expanding human rights, gender equality, and rising intelligence. We can propose ways of acting that increase human flourishing and then test them against these measurable outcomes so that we do not have to rely on personal opinions or inherited wisdom and thus simply repeat the fallacies of the past. However, Pinker adds:

> I don't think we need to be too worried about defining well-being precisely or narrowly. Because I think it is truly open-ended. I mean, there are frontiers of well-being that we may yet discover—or fail to discover, both personally and collectively. We simply don't know how good human life could be. And the concern that gratifying every desire as it arises may not, in fact, be good is simply a concern about the deeper kinds of well-being that could be foreclosed if we lived that way. . . . Certain short-term desires are clearly at odds with deeper, long-term ones. And this is something we all understand. And it can be very difficult to be motivated by long-term desires, where short-term preferences can be gratified. And this is a challenge for living a good life, that we all face.[63]

The only consideration of "next lives" that matters in this discussion is the lives of the people who will inherit the world that we create and how my actions affect the life of the person next to me. There is no heaven, or hell, or nirvana, so no valid appeals can be made to ultimate otherworldly flourishing to trump measurable human flourishing in this world.

It should be possible to agree upon general moral principles so they could be implemented in society and enforced through legal means. This does not mean that these principles should be decided by plebiscite.[64] True flourishing is something that intelligent scientists can define and debate apart from how the general public understands it. Getting the public to believe

---

63. Pinker, Ridley, de Botton, and Gladwell, *Do Humankind's Best Days*, loc. 124–50. Pinker uses these metrics to see if the world is getting better or worse through time.

64. This comment was made by Sam Harris in Flatow, "Can Science."

the truths that science has discovered is more of a political problem than a scientific one. We can eventually expect both progress and agreement in these debates since evolution has given us a shared human nature on which we can base our discussions. As science progresses and helps us to understand ourselves more, we will be better able to predict which actions will lead to actual human flourishing and find better ways to measure and ensure it for the largest number of people. In some respects, this is not so far from some aspects of Aquinas's thinking about morality. He too thinks moral principles will be those that lead to human flourishing, even though he does not take the kind of quantitative approach that Pinker does.

To see how these three different approaches to morality affect the discernment of specific moral principles, we will now look at some specific moral cases. There have been many developments in this thinking since the time of Aquinas and Tsongkhapa, so we will note their own position but also how the tradition that acknowledges their authority views the issue today. We will examine 1) gender equality, 2) homosexuality and gay marriage, and 3) medical research using human embryonic stem cells.

Gender Equality

Thomas Aquinas viewed women as inherently inferior to men. In accord with the science of his day, men provided the seed for a new life and women provided a place for it to grow. Thus, since like produces like, all new life was considered to be inherently male and could eventually grow into the fullness of humanity, an adult male, but sometimes something went wrong and instead the seed became a female, unable to create new seeds.[65] Women were therefore seen as naturally inferior to men and should be subordinate to them within the church and in broader society as well.

Modern science has given us a new view of the differences between the sexes, including the fact that both parents contribute to the genetic makeup of a new life, and that this new life is usually either male or female because it has either an X and a Y chromosome or two X chromosomes.[66] There is no basis therefore to see women as inferior to men. A

---

65. Aquinas, *Summa Theologiae*, 1:92.1 resp. 1.

66. There could also be abnormal chromosome configurations such as two X and one Y chromosome and other problems of development that produce a person of an ambiguous sex. This is a newly recognized phenomenon, so there is not a consensus among natural law theologians about how to think about these situations.

contemporary Catholic centrist position on this issue can be found in the 1988 papal encyclical on women, *Mulieris Dignitatem*. In this document, John Paul II labels viewing women as naturally inferior and thus subordinate to men as sinful and against the Gospel and the natural law. Men and women are equally made in the image of God.[67] When the woman is created from the man's rib, she is instantly recognized as "flesh of his flesh and bone of his bones," his equal in humanity, above all other animals. Yet, "In the 'unity of the two,' man and woman are called from the beginning not only to exist 'side by side' or 'together,' but they are also called to exist mutually 'one for the other.'"[68] This mutual self-gift is disturbed because of original sin, and as a consequence, they quit behaving as equals and men begin to rule over women.[69] Husbands and wives should be equals in a Christian marriage, equally giving themselves to each other and obeying each other in love.[70] That men have traditionally been "head of the household" is a sign of our brokenness, not God's ultimate plan for the world, since it came about as one of the punishments because of the fall. A Christian marriage should be a sign of the Kingdom of God, not of our brokenness. "Parenthood—even though it belongs to both—is realized much more fully in the woman, especially in the prenatal period. It is the woman who 'pays' directly for this shared generation, which literally absorbs the energies of her body and soul."

Women should be treated equally in society as well:

> And what shall we say of the obstacles which in so many parts of the world still keep women from being fully integrated into social, political and economic life? We need only think of how the gift of motherhood is often penalized rather than rewarded, even though humanity owes its very survival to this gift. Certainly, much remains to be done to prevent discrimination against those who have chosen to be wives and mothers. As far as personal rights are concerned, there is an urgent need to achieve real equality in every area: equal pay for equal work, protection for working mothers, fairness in career advancements, equality of spouses with regard to family rights and the recognition of everything that is part of the rights and duties of citizens in a democratic State.[71]

---

67. John Paul II, *Mulieris Dignitatem*, § 6.
68. John Paul II, *Mulieris Dignitatem*, § 7.
69. John Paul II, *Mulieris Dignitatem*, § 9.
70. John Paul II, *Mulieris Dignitatem*, § 18.
71. John Paul II, "Letter to Women," § 4.

However, there are some positions of authority that are denied to women. Priestly ordination is the sacrament that confers leadership within the church, and the Roman Catholic Church believes that it "has no authority whatsoever to confer priestly ordination on women."[72] There are several reasons for this, the most commonly cited are the example of Jesus in only choosing men as apostles and that reserving the priesthood to men has been the constant practice of the church throughout its history.[73] This difference should not be thought of as demonstrating the superiority of men over women, since the priesthood is a position of service to the community, not a career path, and women have their own unique roles to play in the church. "Furthermore, the fact that the Blessed Virgin Mary, Mother of God and Mother of the Church, received neither the mission proper to the Apostles nor the ministerial priesthood clearly shows that the non-admission of women to priestly ordination cannot mean that women are of lesser dignity, nor can it be construed as discrimination against them." And finally, "the greatest in the Kingdom of Heaven are not the ministers but the saints."[74]

Tsongkhapa viewed women as spiritually equal to men in that they can both attain enlightenment, though he accepted their sociological inferiority. Consciousness is not inherently masculine or feminine. All mind-streams live countless lives, some of them will be as women, some of them will be as men. To become enlightened one needs to move beyond the dichotomies of masculine and feminine and integrate and balance these different ways of being.[75] One reason why someone would be born male is because they have developed a desire for male things rather than female things.[76] It is not a higher level of development. However, this spiritual equality has always been lived out in the context of sociological inequality. The Buddha originally only allowed men to be monks and live in community as renunciates. When his aunt Pajapati wanted to become a nun rather than a lay-follower,

---

72. John Paul II, *Ordinatio Sacerdotalis*, § 4.
73. John Paul II, *Ordinatio Sacerdotalis*, § 1.
74. John Paul II, *Ordinatio Sacerdotalis*, § 3.
75. Alan Sponberg identifies four different attitudes toward women in early Buddhist sources in Sponberg, "Attitudes toward Women." Tsongkhapa's view corresponds most closely to the *soteriological androgyny* position.
76. Tsongkhapa, *Great Treatise*, 1:245. One might also be born male for "rescuing those whose male organs will be cut off," but this does not make being male inherently superior or inferior to being female.

he refused.[77] When prevailed upon by his disciple Ananda to admit that women were spiritually equal to men he relented, but added that nuns must always be subordinate to monks, and that because of this compromise, the dharma would survive only five hundred years rather than one thousand. To this day Tsongkhapa's Gelukpa order exhibits the androcentrism that is inherent in the story, with nuns generally subordinate to monks and having less prestige, educational opportunities, and financial support than the monks—though things are beginning to change.

In 2017, the Dalai Lama declared the first Tibetan Women's Day at his home in Dharamsala.[78] During the keynote address he mentioned that women were innately more compassionate and empathetic than men and that the world could use more women in leadership positions. He welcomed the first class of women in modern times to earn the degree of Geshema, the equivalent of a PhD in Buddhist philosophy. He noted that women still cannot gain the highest level of ordination, becoming bhikshuni, only because the lineages of bhikshuni died out long ago and are difficult to reestablish, but he is trying to get them reestablished. Because there is a difference between men and women, to keep the world balanced they should have equal rights and equal opportunities. To underscore this point, in 2015 the Dalai Lama stirred up controversy by repeating a comment of his from fifteen years earlier. When asked by a journalist if his next incarnation might be as a woman, he said that was entirely possible if that is what the world needed, especially since women are naturally more compassionate. He then added jokingly that she would have to be very attractive so that she would have more affect on people. Some considered this remark sexist, setting different standards for men and women. The Dalai Lama simply thought that it was humorous and true.[79]

Gender equality is a signature issue for Steven Pinker, one that he often invokes to gauge the moral development of a society. Societies that have granted more equality to various groups are judged as more advanced. The reason is simple: people dislike being treated unfairly, and it feels unfair to be judged by the average of a group that one might be a part of rather than on one's own merits.[80] Thus, while it may be true that men and women

77. Sponberg, "Attitudes toward Women."

78. Saldon, "His Holiness."

79. Freeman, "Dalai Lama." The Dalai Lama later commented on his quip in Aktuell and Doepke, "Interview."

80. For a concise analysis of his arguments, see Pinker, *Blank Slate*, 145–52.

statistically differ in their ability to perform certain jobs or avail themselves of particular opportunities, it is unfair to judge any particular person based on these statistical differences. It is then reasonable to invoke the Golden Rule and prohibit job discrimination and insure equal opportunities for men and women, just as we have done on the basis of race and religion. The fact that societies have begun to see this and gain sympathy for the plight of women shows progress.

As a practical matter, Pinker notes that it is impossible to completely abandon making choices about individuals based on their group associations. It would take an unlimited of amount resources to find out every bit of information about an individual to make a perfectly individualized decision. Thus, society defines where acceptable limits of discrimination should be. Criteria for these decisions depend upon the amount of perceived overlap between groups and the consequences of misjudging the outcome. If the overlap between different groups is small, we feel more justified in using it to discriminate. For instance, if we tested every chimpanzee in the world we might find a few who would benefit from a kindergarten level education, yet we find it acceptable to limit public funding for education to human children. People are also willing to accept an increasing amount of discrimination as the benefits grow larger. Pinker illustrates this point with two typically American examples:

Most people are appalled by racial profiling—for example, pulling over motorists for "driving while black." But after the 2001 terrorist attacks on the World Trade Center and the Pentagon, about half of Americans polled said they were not opposed to ethnic profiling—scrutinizing passengers for "flying while Arab." People who distinguish the two must reason that the benefits of catching a marijuana dealer do not outweigh the harm done to innocent black drivers, but the benefits of stopping a suicide hijacker do outweigh the harm done to innocent Arab passengers.[81]

Proscribing discrimination against women does not come without a cost. The biological differences between men and women might correlate to real job performance differences, but most Western societies are moving in the direction of accepting those costs for the sake of not causing unfair harm to women. Even though it might be statistically true that more women than men resign from work after having a child, most people in Western societies would think it wrong not to hire a women as a bank manager for this reason, and many countries have laws against it.

81. Pinker, *Blank Slate*, 148.

Steven Pinker and modern Catholics and Gelukpas all believe that there are inherent differences between the sexes, but men and women nonetheless have an equal dignity and humanity. This basic equality has not been embodied in society, and so remains an ideal to be sought after. They each have different reasons for holding this, but basically agree that there is a single human nature that is generally embodied in two different modes, a male and a female mode, but it is the shared human nature that is most important in denoting abilities and conferring rights. Catholics and Gelukpas believe that women are still barred from some positions within religious institutions not because they are inferior but because the requirements for them were set down in a foundational era that has normative value. Those in charge today have a restricted ability to change practices that are historically ancient. Contrarily, Pinker believes that historical precedent is not a probative factor in determining the best way to live. There are also different interpretations of history, and there are people closely aligned to the Catholic and Gelukpa traditions that read that same history differently and believe that there is a warrant to ordain women to leadership positions. Catholics and Gelukpas can also point to fundamental reasons why discrimination between the sexes is wrong. For Pinker, enlightened societies have grown into seeing discrimination against women as wrong, but it is fundamentally a choice that societies make to treat people fairly that is finally being extended to women, and there is no fundamentally convincing reason that sexism is wrong.

Homosexuality and Gay Marriage

Another important area of discussion in contemporary society is in the area of homosexuality: whether homosexual acts are sinful or intrinsically harmful and should be banned; whether or not it is just to discriminate against homosexual persons in employment, housing and access to public services; and whether two people of the same sex have a right to get married or adopt children. There has been a great movement of thought in Western societies in this area over the last forty years, so there is quite a diversity of opinions on the subject.

Aquinas died before he completed the *Summa*, and one part that he had planned but never completed was a consideration of marriage and the role of sex in human life. Thomistic thinkers, following his ideas, have developed detailed accounts and responded to the modern questions of homosexuality and gay marriage.

For Thomists, understanding the morality of acts is partly about understanding their place within a human life. Eating, say, has a biological role of gaining nutriments that enable us to live, grow, and thrive, and also, perhaps, of bringing us together as friends. These are not socially determined roles for food, but are in some sense part of the meaning of food for human beings. Still, we can use eating in other ways: to cheer ourselves up when we are down, to emphasize status by eating expensive and rare foods, to judge others for their refinement by watching how they eat, and so on. Some of these ways of using food run contrary to the natural meaning of food in human society. To use food to emphasize social divisions or to show off is contrary to the natural role food plays in bringing people together. To eat to make myself feel better is part of the natural role food plays in our lives, but at some point, if I continue to eat too much to make up for what is lacking in my life in other ways, I can become overweight and damage my health and well-being, running counter to the natural role food should have in my life.

In a similar way, Thomists have argued that sexual intercourse is by nature for the procreation of the human species.[82] If we use sex in ways that thwart this natural role of procreation, then we act wrongly. Thus, intercourse between members of the same sex is wrong because it is not the kind of sexual act that can in principle procreate children. Marriage is the natural context within which children should be conceived and raised, and so is the only acceptable context for sexual intercourse and can only be between one man and one women. This is the teaching about marriage in the Bible, both Old and New Testaments. Contemporary Catholic teaching has recognized that just as eating has a biological and a social function in human life, so, too, while sexual relations are principally for procreation they are also for promoting the unity of husband and wife.[83]

The Catholic Church teaches that while it is not sinful to be attracted to people of the same sex, and discrimination and violence against homosexuals is wrong, sexual acts between people of the same sex are always sinful.[84] Those who are sexually attracted exclusively to people of the same

---

82. Petri, *Aquinas and the Theology*, 49–51, gives a good overview of the development of Thomistic thinking on the subject, for example.

83. Paul VI, *Humanae Vitae*, § 12.

84. For a short summary of a dominant Catholic view of homosexuality today, see

sex are encouraged to celibacy and others in society are encouraged to support them in this and to maintain their love for them, just as God still loves them. Beyond this, people have rights in society and they do not lose them just because they sin. These rights include the protection of families and the right to inheritance. Since gay people can enter into relationships of commitment and dependence with another person and can have children whom they have a right and need to protect, the state should provide them some kind of legal protection. In 2014, Pope Francis caused a stir by signaling that he was open to discussion in this area, saying, "We have to look at the different cases and evaluate them in their variety."[85] Francis was adamant in refusing to call relationships between people of the same sex *gay marriages*, insisting that they be called *civil unions*, because they are not equivalent to marriage. According to the natural law, a marriage is between one man and one woman. Francis's position hearkened back to a compromise that Archbishop William Levada made in 1997 with the city of San Francisco after the city passed an ordinance to require that *domestic partners* be extended the same health care coverage as spouses. Levada argued:

> I am in favor of increasing benefits, especially health coverage, for anyone. As the Catholic bishops of the U.S. stated in 1993, "Every person has a right to adequate health care." I would welcome the opportunity to work with city officials to find ways to overcome what I believe is a national shame, the fact that so many Americans have no health coverage at all. I can be counted on to raise my voice in support of universal health coverage nationally and locally. I feel sure I could make common cause with city officials in working toward this truly urgent need.
>
> But I reject the notion that it discriminates against homosexual, or unmarried heterosexual, domestic partners if they do not receive the same benefits society has provided to married employees to help maintain their families. If it is a question of benefits, why should not blood relatives, or an elderly person or a child who lives in the same household, enjoy these same benefits? Under the city's new ordinance, however, blood relatives are excluded from the benefits that the city's new ordinance extends to domestic partners.

Levada convinced the city that it was more fair and more just to allow employees to designate anyone that they lived with and were responsible for

---

United States Conference of Catholic Bishops, "Always Our Children."
  85. La Stampa, "Francis."

to be the recipient of spousal equivalent benefits so that people could be helped in caring for their elderly parents or dependent relatives as well. The city codified this interpretation and Levada called it a success, writing, "I am satisfied that in San Francisco we have achieved a notable success by shifting the debate so that what was intended by proponents of the legislation as a requirement that all employers accept an equality of status between domestic partnership and marriage has now become a situation where employers can expand health care benefits, while not being forced to recognize that marriage and domestic partnership are equivalent."[86] Levada, like Francis, refuses to acknowledge the validity of gay marriage, but wants to protect the rights of all people, even those who enter into such unions.

For Steven Pinker, we do not have to take recourse to human nature or biological explanations to combat bigotry against homosexuals. People simply have a "right to engage in private consensual acts without discrimination or harassment."[87] The struggle for equal rights for homosexuals is another example of the many recent Rights Revolutions that have been sweeping modern societies and showing how the world is getting better and more peaceful. Since 1975, there has been a steady decline in the percentage of Americans who believe that homosexual acts are morally wrong. At the same time, Americans have steadily become more in favor of equal opportunities for homosexuals such that in 2010, a majority were in favor of legalizing gay marriage.[88] This has happened as awareness of the presence of homosexuals in our communities and in our families has grown, making it increasingly difficult to keep them outside of our circle of sympathy. This societal change has happened in spite of the prohibition against it in Abrahamic faiths that have ratified some of our worst instincts.[89] "Every human rights organization considers the criminalization of homosexuality to be a human rights violation, and in 2008 in the UN General Assembly, sixty-six countries endorsed a declaration urging that all such laws be repealed."[90] By 2010, homosexuality had been legalized in 120 countries, though it was still against the law in 80 others.

---

86. Levada, "San Francisco Solution."
87. Pinker, *How the Mind Works*, 56.
88. Pinker, *Better Angels*, 448–51.
89. Pinker, *Better Angels*, 475.
90. Pinker, *Better Angels*, 449–50.

In Pinker's view, no one is harmed by homosexual behavior.[91] Humans naturally "now and again seek sexual gratification from all manner of living and nonliving things that don't contribute to their reproductive output." The real puzzles are why it is deemed so offensive and how a tendency toward exclusively homosexual relationships could have evolved. Most societal violence and laws against homosexual activity are against men having sex with other men rather than women having sex with other women. Straight men could be expected to react to gay men by thinking, "Great, that's more women for me!" The fact that they react negatively is puzzling, since they should react far more negatively to lesbianism since it could be thought to deprive them of prospective partners. "These beliefs may be products of the cross-wiring between disgust and morality that leads people to confuse visceral revulsion with objective sinfulness. That short circuit may convert an impulse to avoid homosexual partners into an impulse to condemn homosexuality." There is evidence of a genetic basis for exclusive homosexual orientation, but it is unclear how this could have evolved since homosexual men would have fewer offspring. It could be a secondary effect of some more beneficial mutation, or it could be the result of a natural response to a new social situation that has not had time to be filtered out by evolution.[92]

While the Buddhist Churches of America, an offshoot of Pure Land Buddhism from Japan, began performing same-sex marriages in the 1970s, Tsongkhapa's Gelukpa order has been largely resistant to embracing this change.[93] Tsongkhapa listed sexual misconduct as one of the ten nonvirtuous actions that lead to negative karma: killing, stealing, sexual misconduct, lying, divisive speech, offensive speech, senseless speech, covetousness, malice, and wrong views.[94] Sexual activity can be wrong for four different reasons: it could be with a person you are forbidden to have intercourse with, you could use inappropriate body parts, you could have sex in an inappropriate place, or at an inappropriate time. "Those with whom one should not have intercourse in the case of men are women with whom you should not copulate, all men, and eunuchs." The prohibition against having

---

91. Pinker, *Better Angels*, 448–49.

92. For instance, a mutation that tends toward homosexual orientation in men that was associated with the X chromosome and conferred higher fertility in women could be stronger in women since they have two copies of the X chromosome.

93. For a history and analysis of the Buddhist Churches of America's early move to sanction same-sex marriages see Wilson, "All Beings Equally Embraced."

94. Tsongkhapa, *Great Treatise*, 1:218–27.

sex with men also precludes having sex with oneself.[95] The only appropriate body part for a man's penis to join in intercourse with is a vagina, not a hand or a mouth or any other crevice or orifice. These prohibitions also apply to sexual relationships between married couples.

In all of these areas of nonvirtuous actions, the context is important, so there are situations, such as within particular tantric practices, where generally forbidden sexual activity can have a positive karmic effect. However, these cases are unique exceptions to a generally applicable rule and so are not specified in general texts on the dharma and serve to reinforce the rule, not undermine it.

Today, when asked these same questions by Buddhists in the context of teaching the dharma, the Dalai Lama will repeat Tsongkhapa's prohibitions against homosexual acts verbatim and in full.[96] But he will also add that people should follow the dictates of their own religion, and that "we have to make a distinction between believers and unbelievers. From a Buddhist point of view, men-to-men and women-to-women is generally considered sexual misconduct. From society's viewpoint, mutually agreeable homosexual relations can be of mutual benefit, enjoyable and harmless."[97] While the traditional Buddhist teaching on this point has not changed, its impact is attenuated to include only Buddhists. When asked to clarify his remarks later, the Dalai Lama gave out a press release that said, "His Holiness opposes violence and discrimination based on sexual orientation. He urges respect, tolerance, compassion, and the full recognition of human rights for all.... Since these matters [of sexuality] are complex and require careful consideration, His Holiness welcomes the invitation and suggestion for further study and discussion on human sexuality to be organized by some of the meeting participants."[98] Those at the meeting found the Dalai Lama open and nonjudgmental. He said that it was not his place to reinterpret traditional teachings on his own authority, and he encouraged them to begin conversations and see if they could get a consensus from a broad spectrum of modern Buddhists on reinterpreting these traditional teachings for a modern age.

---

95. Interestingly, Tsongkhapa finds nothing harmful with a man having sex with a woman prostitute, as long as the man pays for it himself and it is mutually agreeable.

96. Gyatso, *Beyond Dogma*, 47.

97. Lattin, "Dalai Lama Speaks."

98. "His Holiness" is a traditional title for the Dalai Lama. The remarks are from a press release put out after the meeting, as found in Harvey, *Introduction*, 433.

Research Using Human Embryonic Stem Cells

When a human egg is fertilized it forms a zygote and begins to divide into two, then four, then eight cells, and so on. This is the blastocyst stage, and all the cells are pluripotent, able to become any type of cell in the body. At a certain stage of development, the fetus becomes organized, moving beyond the blastocyst stage as cells lose their pluripotency and begin to differentiate into specific types and organs. Since pluripotent embryonic stem cells are able to become any type of cell in the body, they are being studied for potential use in regenerative medicine to create synthetic organs, repair tissue damage, and treat degenerative brain conditions such as Alzheimer's disease.

All three of these views believe in protecting human life. As a general principle, all people have a right to life. It is wrong to kill one person to enhance the life of someone else, even if it is to extend the life of the recipient. For this reason it is illegal to take the heart from a living person and give it to someone else, even if the donor agrees. The donor and the recipient each have an equal right to life that must be respected. A heart cannot be removed from a person until he or she has died of natural causes, and one cannot hasten the death of the donor in order to enhance the odds of success of the operation. The same is not true of donating a kidney, since the donor can still live a healthy life, although at a greater risk of future problems. The benefits to the recipient—life itself—are on a different level than the problems caused to the donor—potential future health problems if something happens to their remaining kidney.

The Roman Catholic Church has been adamant in its opposition to research using embryonic stem cells that are obtained through the destruction of embryos. We have already seen that Aquinas taught that a developing human embryo went through a series of substantial changes with a vegetative and an animal soul until it finally received a human soul once it had physically developed enough to support human abilities. Nevertheless, from the moment a sperm and egg unite to form a zygote, a new life has formed with a distinctive human genetic makeup and a development that is self-directed. Whether or not this life is a full human person or a form of human life in its early stages, it "demands the unconditional respect that is morally due to the human being in his bodily and spiritual totality."[99] Thus, it is wrong to destroy a zygote or a blastocyst in

---

99. Roman Catholic Church, *Donum Vitae*, § 1.4.

order to obtain stem cells for any reason, and one cannot use stem cells that have come from these sources without becoming complicit in the immoral destruction of life. There are other sources of stem cells besides taking them from living embryos, destroying them in the process. There are a certain number of embryonic stem cells in the placenta and in amniotic fluid, and adult stem cells can be obtained from bone marrow, brain, and other tissues. There is no moral prohibition to obtaining stem cells by methods that do not cause serious harm to the subject from whom the stem cells are taken, and the church encourages research into therapeutic treatments using these stem cells.[100]

Contrarily, Steven Pinker, like other naturalists, does not believe that zygotes and other forms of developing human life deserve the same moral respect and protection as fully developed human persons:

> Who says the doctrine of the soul is more humane than the understanding of the mind as a physical organ? I see no dignity in letting people die of hepatitis or be ravaged by Parkinson's disease when a cure may lie in research on stem cells that religious movements seek to ban because it uses balls of cells that have made the "ontological leap" to "spiritual souls." Sources of immense misery such as Alzheimer's disease, major depression, and schizophrenia will be alleviated not by treating thought and emotion as manifestations of an immaterial soul but by treating them as manifestations of physiology and genetics.[101]

For Pinker, the problem with a doctrine of an immaterial soul is that it artificially elevates some bits of matter above others, investing them with primal attributes of the sacred. It is artificial, because the immaterial soul has no basis in reality. It cannot be tested for, or affect the material world in any way, so why should it affect our ethics? Any trade-offs with the sacred are considered taboo, so there can be no intelligent balancing of competing goods concerning living persons and their needs and pre-human tissues invested with an immaterial soul.

Pinker believes that a better basis for evaluating the morality of the question is suffering and flourishing. "To the extent that we agree on that, it's a scientific and empirical question: Who suffers under what circumstances? Does a conceptus, a fused egg and sperm, have the ability to suffer because it's conscious? Does a person who has a lack of brain activity? Those

---

100. Roman Catholic Church, *Dignitatis Personae*, § 32.
101. Pinker, *Blank Slate*, 189.

are questions in cognitive neuroscience, and the answer very much affects whether euthanasia or abortion or stem cell research is justified."[102]

The Dalai Lama has also been supportive of stem cell research, explaining, "The Buddhist approach is to distinguish generally between sentient and nonsentient beings. There is no distinction made systematically, in the scientific sense, between nonliving and living organisms."[103] Any living being that has a sophisticated enough nervous system to feel pain and pleasure is considered to be sentient,[104] and so animals belong to one of the six realms that participate in karmic-driven rebirth. When a human embryo is developing in the womb, it does not become sentient until its nervous system has sufficiently developed.[105] In commenting on the ethics of stem cell research in 2002, the Dalai Lama said:

> On the questions about stem cell research, I am thinking about the issue of when an embryo becomes sentient from the Buddhist point of view. The Abhidharma texts mention that consciousness enters the embryo through the meeting of the regenerative substances of the father and mother, and at that point it becomes a sentient being. The term that is used implies that, at that point, the embryo is becoming a human. From the classical Buddhist standpoint, it has become a sentient being and extermination of that would be morally equivalent, almost, to killing a human being.
>
> But how do we understand at what point consciousness enters the embryo? This is problematic. A fetus, which is becoming a human is already a sentient being. But a fertilized egg may actually split into 8, 16, 32, 64 cells and become an embryo, and yet be naturally aborted and never become a human being. This is why I feel that for the formation of life, for something to actually become a human, something more is needed than simply a fertilized egg. It may be that what you do to a conglomeration of cells that have the

---

102. Flatow, "Can Science."

103. Luisi, *Mind and Life*, 101.

104. Luisi, *Mind and Life*, 161.

105. For a longer explanation tying this process to the twelve-linked chain of causation, see the Introduction by Jeffrey Hopkins in Gyatso, *Meaning of Life*, 13–18. In the third link of the chain, consciousness causes a *new birth*, entering into a space where copulation is happening and becoming enmeshed due to causes and conditions accrued in previous lives. The reincarnated mind-stream causes a new body to begin to grow in the fourth link, *name and form*. Then, in the fifth link the *senses* develop in the new fetus. It is not until the sixth link, *contact*, that the newly developed sense consciousnesses are sufficiently developed to interact with the previous mind-stream and full contact between the mind-stream and the new life occurs.

possibility of becoming human entails no negative or karmically unwholesome act. However, when you're dealing with a configuration of cells that are definitely on the track to becoming a human being, it's a different situation.

In some areas, Buddhism may have a different perspective from secular ethics. I think for example about human rights. From the Buddhist viewpoint, it is very difficult to claim that we human beings have special rights that are categorically different from animal rights. All sentient beings, all beings who have the experience of pain and pleasure, have the natural right to protect their existence and fulfill their aspiration to overcome suffering and enjoy happiness. The claim to rights is based on the capacity to experience pain and pleasure; it has nothing to do with intelligence, which is the main distinction between animals and human beings. They have the same experiences of pain and pleasure that we do.[106]

The ethical question is if a blastocyst has a right to exist that is on par with the right to life or the right to health of a fully formed human person. If not, where is the line? Is it once the fetus has developed a nervous system able to feel pain and pleasure? Is it when the developing fetus is sufficiently formed so that it could survive outside the womb? Is it at birth? Our various authors do not agree, and have good reasons for their differences.

Conclusions

Thomas Aquinas, Tsong-kha-pa Blo-bzang-grags-pa, and Steven Pinker have very different views of what it means to be human, what is real, and what it means to act ethically. Perhaps Pinker's view of the human is simplest, since he does not believe in a soul or in an afterlife. Human persons are just their bodies. They think with their brains and when their bodies die, they cease to exist. But human consciousness and free will are mysteries that are perhaps unknowable, and since this is such a constitutive part of being human, we can say that, for Pinker, the human person is still an enigma. Tsongkhapa believed that we have bodies that are as real as anything else in the universe, but that the consciousness of any one of us not only predated our body, it existed before the universe was created. If we wanted to choose either our uncreated consciousness or this body to which it is bound to call our true self, we would be reminded that there is no self, and the dichotomous thinking that leads us to choose one or

---

106. Gyatso, "When Does a Stem Cell," 15.

the other is our beginningless nescience working itself out. What we really are cannot be put into words and limited by concepts, but it can be experienced. Aquinas believed that humans were body-soul composites, with souls so united to our bodies that they are the basis of our existence. Yet God also endows humans with an immaterial aspect to their souls such that they can understand and love and have free choice, and because of this, human souls do not cease to exist when their bodies die. But existence without a body is not what we were made for, so God can raise us from the dead and give us new life with bodies that are the same and different, since they will be ours but also incorruptible.

For Pinker, the world that we experience is the real world. There is certainly more to our world than what we experience, since our senses are limited, but we have no indication that any other world exists, particularly any supernatural realm. While humans throughout history have believed in supernatural realms and divine beings, they were mistaken. Modern science has enabled us to understand how these mistakes were able to persist and be perpetuated, and it has also allowed us to see that religious beliefs in enchantments and gods are not true. Moving forward, we can trust science to help us forge a better future based on reality, rather than on the ignorance of religious superstitions and holy writ. The best way to ground public morality is to determine numerical metrics that measure human flourishing and then let social scientists determine which actions actually maximize the parameters.

For Tsongkhapa, the world we experience is the world we have to deal with, but it is not ultimately real. By following a qualified teacher, we can be guided through a series of meditations and philosophical analyses of our experience that will allow us to see through our delusion and experience a deeper reality, enlightenment. Enlightenment will not reveal to us another place or a simple escape from existence; it will free us to engage this world in an effective, unlimited, and unrestricted way that is not only impossible for us right now, but which we now believe to be absolutely impossible. We can expect the world to become better and suffering to lessen as more and more people adopt Buddhist teachings and begin to work more effectively to end the suffering of all sentient beings. The basis of morality is found in the Noble Eightfold Path and the writings of great teachers who spell out how to do no harm and be a benefit to others, but it can also be known by anyone willing to think through actions and their consequences.

For Aquinas, the world we experience was created by God in order to share his infinite love and it is held in being in every moment by God who is existence itself. We are the capstones of physical creation, made in God's image with the ability to know and love, set here to care for creation. Ultimately, we will find our fulfillment in heaven where we will see God "face-to-face" with bodies that no longer suffer pain or sickness. God has made this possible through the incarnation, death, and resurrection of his Son, Jesus Christ, and has established the church in order to carry on Jesus's work and proclaim this Good News to the world. So we can expect the world to become better as more and more people hear the message of Jesus Christ and begin to live according to God's plan. The basis of morality is found in the natural law, which can be known through observing and thinking about the world, but morality also needs to be guided by revelation because not everyone has the time to study philosophy and errors can be made. Further, humans need to cultivate the virtues, skills for living well, since no laws adequately capture the complexity of human morality.

These differences of opinion about what is real and what is right lead to differences in opinions on specific moral norms. Modern followers of all three agree that men and women are inherently of equal value and dignity and should have equal career opportunities, but Gelukpas and Catholics believe they are justified in proscribing women from essential areas of leadership within their communities. Gelukpas and Catholics are also agreed in proscribing homosexual acts as intrinsically evil while Pinker sees them as statistically normal for a certain percentage of the population. All three agree that society should protect homosexual individuals from discrimination and violence, but Pinker believes that giving homosexuals full and equal rights in society is a sign of progress, while the Catholic Church is against allowing homosexual marriage in civil society. Buddhists are still trying to find a consistent position on this issue. Finally, Pinker and the Dalai Lama agree that using embryonic stem cells to combat disease is a good thing, while the Catholic Church is adamantly opposed to it. Pinker and the Dalai Lama base their reasoning on the fact that these early forms of developing cells are not human and cannot feel pain and so are not entitled to the same protections as do human beings, while the Catholic Church believes that even early forms of life are genetically human and deserve the benefit of the doubt and the same protections as any human person.

The differences in these various positions are profound and do not seem amenable to reconciliation in the foreseeable future.

5

Learning from Others

In previous chapters we have seen the differing pictures of the world painted by Thomas Aquinas, Tsongkhapa, and Steven Pinker and we have compared and contrasted them. In this chapter we will explore how one might learn by looking at these various pictures together through a process of comparative theology. Each of us has a picture of the world that aids us in successfully negotiating our day-to-day environment. Perhaps we have not thought through the details of our picture the way that Aquinas, Tsongkhapa, and Pinker have, but our pictures of the world just as surely guide our thinking and acting. It is therefore useful to examine our own world-picture and our beliefs to see if we might like to improve them or extend them a bit.

Our world-picture provides the context for our thinking, including how we evaluate what is true and what is good.[1] We cannot simply choose a new world-picture or create one out of whole cloth because we would have no basis for deciding which one to choose without employing a particular world-picture. But our world-picture can evolve and change, so it behooves us to help it to grow in a direction that conforms more closely to the world we experience so that we can think about the world better and make better decisions. We have each built our current world-picture through a lifetime of experiences and learning and thinking about the world. Hopefully through more learning and having more experiences and spending more time thinking about these things we can improve our world-picture.

A good way to improve one's world-picture is to examine it in light of world-pictures that are significantly different from our own. This book has outlined three radically different world-pictures to allow readers to see

---

1. See the introduction, pp. xv–xvi, for an explanation of world-pictures.

just how different they can be and to allow readers to reflect on how their own views might be represented within this diversity. If we were to judge the overall validity of world-pictures that were radically different from our own, we would almost certainly judge them to be wrong and could probably explain exactly why they were wrong. By our criteria for validity—which is based in our world-picture—these other views would be seen as erroneous or at least deficient. It seems unlikely that Aquinas, upon learning the Buddhist concept of *maya*, would be convinced of its truth and abandon his own critical realism. It seems unlikely that Pinker would be convinced that God exists by pondering Aquinas's argument for the substantial immateriality of the human soul. But each of these thinkers has learned some things from others who believe quite differently than they do. Aquinas is a shining example. Aquinas studied the Greek philosopher Aristotle as he had been remembered through Islamic philosophers, and brought much of Aristotle's thought into his Christian world-picture. The main features were left behind of course. Aquinas did not begin to believe in the validity of Greek gods, or no gods, or in the prophet Muhammad. Aquinas was criticized for bringing "pagan" ideas into Christianity, but in the end, he created such a powerful vision of Christianity that it eventually predominated.

In this chapter we will do as Aquinas did—reconsider the Christian tradition under the influence of good ideas from outside the tradition, allowing Buddhist and naturalist considerations to indicate where there might be weaknesses in our current understanding. This is an approach called for by Pope John Paul II when writing:

> The hylomorphism of Aristotelian natural philosophy, for example, was adopted by the medieval theologians to help them explore the nature of the sacraments and the hypostatic union. This did not mean that the Church adjudicated the truth or falsity of the Aristotelian insight, since that is not her concern. It did mean that this was one of the rich insights offered by Greek culture, that it needed to be understood and taken seriously and tested for its value in illuminating various areas of theology. Theologians might well ask, with respect to contemporary science, philosophy and the other areas of human knowing, if they have accomplished this extraordinarily difficult process as well as did these medieval masters.[2]

---

2. John Paul II, "Letter of His Holiness."

In response to John Paul II, our task here is to see if we can allow the rich thought of Buddhism and naturalism to illumine various areas of contemporary Catholic belief as well as did the medieval masters. The authors of this book are both Catholic theologians, so it is their vocation to improve Christian theology. Contemporary Buddhists and naturalistic philosophers might consider using this same material to improve their own views, but we will leave that task to them.

This chapter is speculative theology. Rather than simply documenting what Catholic Christians have believed in the past, this chapter explores ways in which Catholic beliefs might change in the future. There are reasons to resist such changes, some of which will be pointed out, but since Catholics believe that God is Truth itself and that all truth is ultimately unified and reconcilable, Catholic theologians are encouraged to seek truth wherever it is to be found—even in Buddhism and naturalism. In the end, perhaps the changes we will explore here will ultimately be judged as invalid by the Catholic Church, and in that case we will happily renounce them as well. We intend to improve Catholic theology, not depart from it. But for now, let us speculate about where greater insight into truth lies, by looking at three different areas within Christian theology: original sin and our need for salvation; the extent of the salvation won by Jesus Christ; and the Christian vision of heaven.

Original Sin and Our Need for Salvation

Our first topic is about the fundamental Catholic teaching of *original sin*—that all people are born with disordered passions such that they are inclined to sin. The doctrine has roots in the second creation story in the Bible's book of Genesis, the creation of Adam and Eve in the Garden of Eden. In this story, Adam and Eve, the first humans, lived an idyllic life and wanted for nothing. They ate of the fruit of the trees of the Garden, but they were not allowed to eat the fruit of the tree in the center of the Garden. However, a serpent convinced Eve that it would be good to eat this forbidden fruit, so she did, and gave some to Adam who ate it as well. Because of this transgression, Adam and Eve were banished from the Garden, lost their harmonious relationship to the world and to each other, and forevermore had to struggle to find food to survive. This is often referred to as *the fall*. In the New Testament, Paul, in his Letter to the Romans, asserts that all were made sinners in Adam's sin, just as all could be saved by the work of Christ.[3] How a sinful act of Adam caused the rest of humanity to contract this state of disorder has never been settled.

Classical Views of Augustine and Aquinas

Two important theories about original sin are found in the works of Augustine of Hippo and Thomas Aquinas. In Augustine's account, Adam is seen as God's servant who disobeyed God's commandment.[4] As a result, Adam's own body, which should be his servant, became disobedient in its central function of procreation. While his hands and feet, arms and legs were still under the control of his will, his genitals were not. These were moved by lust, acting and not acting often against his will. As these are used in creating new life, new life that sprang from him inherited this brokenness, and thus has it been down to our own day. All people are conceived through inordinate, unruly lust rather than through reason, so all contract original sin. All except for Jesus, of course, who was born of the Virgin, without a human father, and so was conceived without sin. This inordinate human lust that moves men's genitals is called *concupiscence*, and it is the root of original sin in us.

Thomas Aquinas conceived of this differently. Aquinas argued that before the fall, Adam's will was perfectly aligned with God's will by a special help given to him by God called *original justice*.[5] Because of Adam's sin, God stopped giving this extra grace to Adam, and Adam's will fell into disorder. One effect of this disorder is concupiscence, but there are many others, such as an ignorance of God's will. God would have held Adam's posterity in original justice as well, but in removing it from Adam, God removed it from Adam's posterity and thus we are all born in the state of original sin. For Aquinas, the loss of original justice is the root of original sin.

Like Augustine, Aquinas believed that original sin was propagated through men and not women, leaving Jesus free from original sin, but for a different reason. While Augustine thought that original sin came from a disordered sexual act that was necessarily tainted by the man's lust rebelling against his will, Aquinas believed that it might be possible to conceive

---

3. Rom 5:19.
4. Augustine, *On Marriage*, 1: chap. 7 and 27.
5. Aquinas, *Summa Theologiae*, 1–2:83.3 and 1–2:82.3 resp. 2–3.

of a child without lust.[6] Aquinas, like his contemporaries, did not believe that mammalian reproduction came from the joining of a sperm from the father and an egg from the mother. Rather, the male's seminal fluid was the active principle of reproduction, containing seeds with the complete essence of new life, and the woman passively received this fluid, giving it a place to grow, much as a seed needs the earth in order to grow. Thus, Adam passes along his potential to have a disordered will to his posterity, and God does not prevent their wills from indeed becoming disordered.

Both Augustine and Aquinas presuppose that there was an actual sin of the first man, Adam, that caused him to fall into a state of sin, a state that was subsequently propagated to the rest of humanity except Jesus—who did not have a human father—all of whom were Adam's physical descendants. The *Catechism of the Catholic Church*, when speaking of how to interpret the account of the fall states, "The account of the fall in Genesis 3 uses figurative language, but affirms a primeval event, a deed that took place at the beginning of the history of man. Revelation gives us the certainty of faith that the whole of human history is marked by the original fault freely committed by our first parents."[7] But what if there were no single man from whom all of humanity descended? Would there be no first sin whose effects would propagate to all of humanity? It was just this reasoning that led Pope Pius XII to argue in his 1950 papal encyclical *Humani Generis* against polygenesis, the theory that there was more than one single couple from whom all modern humans descended.[8] This did not, however, end the debate.

A Contribution from the Science of Evolution

As Steven Pinker relates, the modern theory of evolution predicts that it is highly unlikely that all surviving members of *Homo sapiens* were descended from one single couple. This is not how evolution works. The species *Homo sapiens* itself would have begun with fuzzy edges, with a certain amount of diversity among its members, some of whom could mate and others not. For instance, imagine three subspecies of early *Homo sapiens*, A, B, and C, each subspecies with its own amount of internal diversity, but genetically and behaviorally close enough to be easily able to produce fertile offspring.

---

6. Aquinas, *Summa Theologiae*, 1–2:82.4 resp. 3.
7. Roman Catholic Church, *Catechism*, § 390.
8. Pius XII, *Humani Generis*, § 37.

Members of subspecies B might be able to mate with most of the members of subspecies A and C as in figure 5.1.

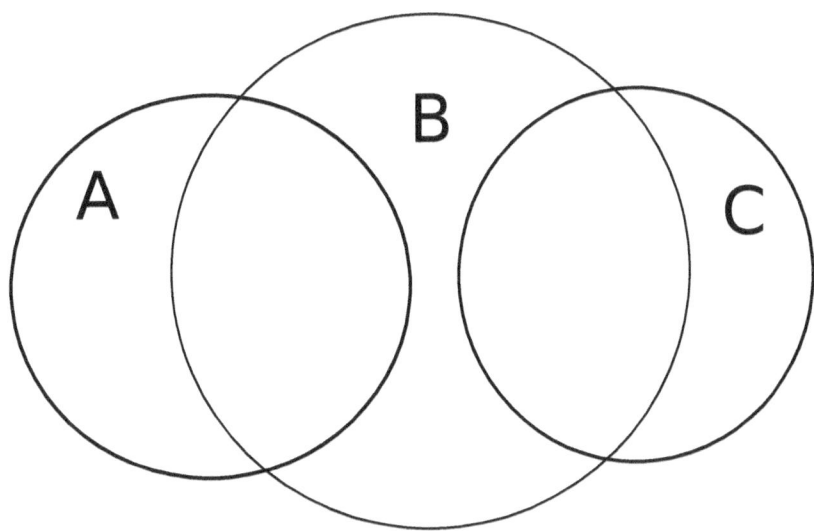

Subspecies A, B, and C within a larger population. Individuals within each subspecies can successfully interbreed. Overlapping zones represent fertile interbreeding between subspecies.

But perhaps none of the members of subspecies A could successfully produce fertile offspring with members of subspecies C. Where one would draw the line of the species is rather arbitrary. From the perspective of subspecies B, the species might include both subspecies A and C. From the perspective of A, C is clearly a different species.

In a 1996 address to the Pontifical Academy of Science, Pope John Paul II stated, "Today, more than a half-century after the appearance of [*Humani Generis*] some new findings lead us toward the recognition of evolution as more than an hypothesis."[9] The convergence of ideas it has brought to independent studies across many different disciplines is a significant argument in its favor. However, there are some limits to how we can understand evolution in light of our faith. Most importantly, while we can look to evolution to explain the origins of our bodies, we need to hold that each individual spiritual soul is created directly by God to explain the dignity of the human person.

---

9. John Paul II, "Message Pontifical Academy."

We cannot "regard the spirit either as emerging from the forces of living matter, or as a simple epiphenomenon of that matter."

Various proposals have been put forth to try to understand evolution in light of the Catholic faith. Nicanor Austriaco has noted that while *Humani Generis* argued against polygenesis, it did not rule it out completely, arguing instead that it was simply not apparent how polygenesis could be reconciled with our understanding of original sin.[10] He then pointed out that the Vatican's own International Theological Commission in 2004 published a theological statement that was open to polygenism. Following this lead, Austriaco has proposed a way of understanding original sin that was faithful to the tradition and open to polygenism. When the *Homo* line had eventually produced individuals with the complete genetic package of pro-language genes, God would have given these individuals substantial immaterial souls, such as humans have and other living things do not, not even the parents of these individuals.[11] God would also have given them the support of original justice. When these individuals would have reached the age of reason, they would have been given the chance to choose to follow God's will fully or to deviate from it, continuing on in original justice or falling into a state of sin that they would pass on to their descendants as original sin. If there were a single couple who received human souls, it would have worked as in the book of Genesis. If there would have been a small population of such individuals in a local area, the actual sin of one could easily have been spread to the group in the same way that Eve led Adam into sin. In either case, the advantages of having the full complement of pro-language genes would have given the offspring of this couple or this small group an evolutionary advantage over their closely related but not humanly ensouled relatives such that they would eventually prevail and thus become the ancestors of all surviving members of *Homo sapiens*.

Austriaco's solution explains how we could hold to the propagation of original sin to all of humanity from a single, freely chosen act in a way that plausibly fits with the findings of the science of evolution, but it raises more questions than it solves. If there was a small band of first generation humans, was there not one who could resist the temptation? This is more plausible when there are only two people, less so if we imagine fifty. Next, is it scientifically plausible that the specific combination of genes that caused God to ensoul certain proto-humans was so beneficial that every proto-human

10. Austriaco, "Historicity," part 1.
11. Austriaco, "Historicity," part 4.

who did not get it eventually died out? If this is so, the largest group that could be the founding of Homo sapiens would be limited to the number of people who could have had direct contact and negatively influenced each other after they gained "the age of reason" yet before any of them procreated. Otherwise, we would have a generation of ensouled humans born without original sin, something that is against the doctrine of original sin. This is possible, but it seems unlikely. It is also logically possible, though unlikely, that God chose a population with genetic diversity to endow with immaterial souls and that receiving these immaterial souls gave them such a reproductive advantage that they supplanted all of their almost genetically identical cousins whom did not receive immaterial souls. Or perhaps God gave ongoing material help to those he endowed with immaterial souls to allow them to out-compete all others, but this also seems unlikely since God did not even do this for his chosen people the Israelites.

Here is a different solution, inspired by Pinker's use of Salvadore Dali's *Raphaelesque Exploding Head* as a metaphor for the human person as created by evolution. We are an assemblage of various components that yield various evolutionary advantages. The unity we find within ourselves is not the unity of top-down design that specifies the working of smaller components so as to further an overarching plan. We are not like fine watches. Rather, we consist of a haphazard alliance of various parts that are constantly being improved and repurposed in response to the changing environment around us, like the swirling pieces that make up the Raphaelesque Head. If you step back, you can see the overarching pattern, but look closely and you can also see the chaos. This is how evolution makes complex organisms. If we picture our minds to be unified information processors, we can imagine their generally smooth and consistent operation. If we picture our minds as composed of different subsystems for evaluating different aspects of reality, such as one system for intuitive physics, another for intuitive biology, and yet another for dealing with tools, we can imagine that they would often clash, especially in situations that were quite different than the norms from our evolutionary past. Aquinas pictures the former, Pinker the latter, and if we accept that our bodies were created through a long process of evolution, Pinker's view makes more sense.

The disorder we sense within ourselves is coded into our DNA and is a necessary product of the process of evolution by which our bodies were created. God is the author of the universe and director of evolution, but the tool that God used to create us left its mark. If our bodies (and brains) developed because of natural selection, we should expect them to be in a state of disordered passions and confused understanding as described in the doctrine of original sin. We can still trace back humanity's universal condition of original sin to specific actions freely chosen by our ancestors, but we don't have to suppose the bad decisions to have been improbable and singular. Rather, we would expect our first ancestors to be continually making sub-optimal choices.

In line with Aquinas's view of humans being made in the image of God, the most significant difference between proto-humans and true humans is the presence of an immaterial soul, allowing for the ability to know and to love. It is this difference that gives humans their inherent value. Humans are never a means to an end, they are ends in themselves. God created the world in order share the divine life, and humans' ability to know God's plan and reflect God's love place them at the pinnacle of creation. If humans' bodies evolved from non-human proto-ancestors, we would not expect the very first true humans to be markedly different physically from their non-human parents except for minutely crossing a threshold of brain and nervous system development to support the ability to know and to love. We have no reason to believe that proto-humans had the ability to live forever, and thus we would have no reason to believe that the first humans would have had the physical ability to live forever. Their bodies would have aged and died.

Perhaps the right way to read these passages is as talking about the peculiar character of human death. Certainly, from one perspective, death seems very different for humans and for other animals. With the other animals, in death nature takes what it granted in birth, but if Christians are right that humans uniquely have free will, then they make their own lives at least to some extent, so that death takes more than nature grants, it takes away the artistry of their lives. So perhaps it is not simply prejudice to think that while the death of other animals is sad and sometimes regrettable, human death is properly the subject of mourning, and even tragedy. In this way, human death is akin to punishment. On this view, the Scriptures give us these stories of the fall partly to explain the strange character of human death. Just like the view of death as metaphor for struggle, this *uniqueness* view sees death *per se* as in some sense natural, built into our genetic makeup, but tragic nonetheless.

There is a long history of people imagining life in the Garden of Eden as being exempt from physical death. The logic is that since Adam and Eve had not sinned they would not die and would live forever. The biblical account asserts that they are not to eat of the tree of the knowledge of good and evil or they would die (Gen 2:15). Paul, in his Letter to the Romans, asserts that death entered into the world through Adam's sin (Rom 5:12). But if our bodies were created through the process of evolution, the death spoken of in the biblical record must be metaphorical and not actual physical death. A limited lifespan is part of our genetic makeup. Interpreting the punishment of death as metaphorical certainly accords with the Genesis narrative, since when Adam and Eve ate of the fruit, they did not immediately die. Rather, life became difficult, childbearing became painful, they had to work to find food, and their relationships with each other and with the world became problematic. These are all apt metaphors for death metaphorically encroaching on life.

If the first humans born with immaterial souls did not live inordinately longer lives than their cousins born without immaterial souls, humanity's time "in the Garden of Eden" had to be shorter than the lifespan of a protohuman, or these first humans would have been born and died without sinning. Perhaps we should think of this as a metaphorical time rather than a historical one. Perhaps there was no actual time when humans existed in an idyllic state, free from disease and distress, free from wants and cares. This would re-center the story of Adam and Eve on explaining the condition we find ourselves in, rather than accounting for how we got here. We find ourselves in a world with so much promise, but that always disappoints. We find ourselves with a great capacity to love, which is often subverted by our tendency to hate. We find ourselves conflicted about which is the better path to take, confused by competing goods and emotions and hampered by a mind that cannot quite sort it all out.

Buddhism and Beginningless Nescience

The evolutionary view that humans have always had this conflict between different subsystems built into them by the evolutionary process fits very well with the condition that Buddhists describe as *beginningless nescience*—that we are somehow confused and ultimately dissatisfied with the world, and this is just a fact of our existence that has always been true since before the beginning of time. How we got this way we do not know, we can simply see that it is true.

Original sin seems like something broken, because we realize that there is also a part of us that says "this should not be" and envisions and even glimpses a more perfect world. There is a current in modern Christianity that is uncomfortable with the idea of original sin, but that we are all in the state of original sin seems to be an obvious truth and a point of connection with Buddhism. Buddhists and Catholics agree that we are broken not in the sense that we are less perfect than we once were, but in the sense that we are not yet all that we can be. Perhaps "unfinished" is a better word to describe ourselves.

But let us not forget the inherent connection between original sin, which is a condition that affects us all, and actual sin, choosing free actions that are contrary to the will of God. How is it that we use "sin" for both? Original sin has its roots in the sin of Adam. But original sin also inclines people to commit actual sins. The modern Thomist Herbert McCabe, who developed a view of the fall very much like the one above, argued that the effect of original sin became most clear in the crucifixion of Jesus.[12] In crucifying Jesus, who was God among us, humans showed that their inner turmoil ultimately involved a rejection of God. What we see in the crucifixion of Jesus is that this state of interior struggle that we call original sin is not just unfortunate, it is sinful, leading inexorably to a rejection of God. In Buddhism it is also clear that nescience leads us to commit actions that are against our own and others' interests, causing negative repercussions and unfortunate rebirths because of the laws of karma. Nescience may be a fact of life, but it is not a neutral fact, and it is intrinsically connected with past and future wrong actions.

This nonhistorical interpretation of Genesis is in line with Catholic views of biblical interpretation, which recognizes that different methods of interpretation are required for different kinds of writings. The question is where to draw the line between historical and figurative elements within the book of Genesis, and this question has been under discussion for a long time. The medieval Dominican theologian Meister Eckhart taught that the story of the Garden of Eden should be understood figuratively rather than literally as a parable that teaches: "First, nature of things; second, the nature of our intellect and how it knows; and third, moral instruction regarding every man's escape from or fall into sin, as well as the punishments that lead sinners back to virtue and virtue's Lord."[13] This

---

12. McCabe, *God Still Matters*, chap. 15.
13. Eckhart, *Essential Sermons*, 108. In justifying this interpretation, Eckhart pointed

is the story of every person's struggle with sin rather than something that happened long ago. The *Catechism of the Catholic Church* seems to draw the line in asserting that there was an "original fault freely committed by our first parents."[14] The interpretation put forth here affirms this insight while moving away from literally interpreting other elements of the story, such as that there ever was a time when life was easy. Life has always been a struggle, and when humanity gained the ability to reason and to love, it used these tools in the struggle for survival as well. This is also the underlying truth of the Buddhist doctrine of beginningless nescience. There never was a time when we were without confusion and without suffering. We began in this universe in nescience and have been struggling to overcome it through countless generations.

Conclusions

Returning to Augustine and Aquinas's pictures of how original sin gets propagated, Aquinas's view seems better. Augustine believed that something in us changed due to the first sin of Adam. Before the fall, Adam had complete control of his own body. After the fall, he could not control his genitals as they were now controlled by unbridled lust. It is difficult to imagine how that could square with evolution or anything we know of modern biology. The desire to procreate is one of many desires that are biologically programmed into mammals to enhance the survival of the species. Lust is a biological advantage, and as such, is part and parcel of the bodies that evolution gave us, not something that was added on after we became human. In contrast, Aquinas believed that nothing in our nature changed because of the fall, we simply cannot operate perfectly without extra grace given by God, extra grace that is no longer given because we have shown that we do not want it. Aquinas's view of the propagation of original sin fits easily with modern views of evolution.

To view original sin as a universal condition of humanity rather than a literal punishment for an historical event would be a change in the way

---

out that Augustine read this story allegorically, and doing so solves problems such as how a woman could speak with a serpent.

14. Roman Catholic Church, *Catechism*, § 390: "The account of the fall in Genesis 3 uses figurative language, but affirms a primeval event, a deed that took place at the beginning of the history of man. Revelation gives us the certainty of faith that the whole of human history is marked by the original fault freely committed by our first parents."

we picture the story of the Garden of Eden, but it would not be a change in doctrine. Rather than as a quasi-historical account of a time of original bliss and harmony, this story is best understood as a parable of the condition we find ourselves in—blessed and broken, created by God for a perfection that we can glimpse but never fully grasp in this world, because of disharmony deep inside ourselves. There is no one other than ourselves to blame for this disharmony, and without God's help, we could never overcome it. But such has it always been, and such is the nature of humans, who cannot live perfectly without the grace of God. We can imagine God giving this extra help and call it original justice, but if we are honest, we know that every one of us turns from God's plan to follow our own path, as we see in the metaphor of eating the forbidden fruit.

Coming to terms with who we are, we see that we should not blame someone in the past for our troubles, nor should we blame God. Original sin describes all of humanity, throughout history. There was no time when humanity lived in harmony with creation in a Garden of Eden, and the story of the Garden of Eden tells us why—because we humans would never live within those boundaries. We can hold to the received doctrine's understanding that original sin proceeds from an original act of turning away from God and is inherited by all, because we can see that the act of turning away from perfection is something we each do many times a day. Evolutionary scientists can provide evidence of this and theories as to why we developed as we did, and Buddhists can concur that it is a fundamental condition of sentient beings.

Contrarily, picturing our idyllic life in the Garden made it clear that we were meant for better things than what we experience now. God intended humans to be his friends, and the rift between humanity and God is the result of human choice to be less than our best selves. If we give an evolutionary account of the doctrine of original sin, how do we avoid making human alienation from God something divinely intended? As Austriaco pointed out, it is against the Catholic tradition to assert that "sin flows from human nature as God had intentionally created it: God made human beings naturally prone to sin."[15] The view put forth here comes dangerously close to this without crossing the line, but an argument against it on this point could be made.

The more traditional picture also gives a clear way of interpreting biblical passages that see Jesus as the new Adam (Rom 5:19, for example).

---

15. Austriaco, "Theological Fittingness," 665.

Can these be reinterpreted so as not to necessitate Adam being an actual, singular human person, perhaps reading the actions of Adam as an image of errors that beset all humans, including the first humans, and Christ as a person who finally overcame these errors by his obedience?

The Extent of the Salvation Won by Jesus Christ

In Catholic understanding, original sin marks the beginning of the history of salvation, but it is not the end. In response to original sin, God worked throughout human history to rescue humanity and bring it to its ultimate destiny to be with God in heaven. As explained in the *Catechism of the Catholic Church*, "This perfect life with the Most Holy Trinity—this communion of life and love with the Trinity, with the Virgin Mary, the angels and all the blessed—is called 'heaven.' Heaven is the ultimate end and fulfillment of the deepest human longings, the state of supreme, definitive happiness."[16] Extending original justice was not an option after humanity freely chose to act against God's will. Salvation requires a free choice to want to move away from sin and self-centeredness toward God and the love of neighbor.[17] God would never force people to be saved against their will.

The center of God's saving work in history is the incarnation, life, death, and resurrection of Jesus Christ. The papal constitution *Benedictus Deus* on the beatific vision, the face-to-face vision of God in heaven given to the saved, pictures the passion and death of Jesus as the fulcrum of salvation.[18] Those who are worthy and who died before it enter the beatific vision at that time. Those who die after it require the sacrament of baptism. Paul, in the Letter to the Romans, explains, "For there is no distinction, since all have sinned and fall short of the glory of God; they are now justified by his grace as a gift, through the redemption that is in Christ Jesus, whom God put forward as a sacrifice of atonement by his blood, effective through faith" (Rom 3:23–25, NRSV). The doctrine of original sin covers the first part of this passage, that all have sinned and thus do not merit heaven. The second half speaks of God's ultimate remedy of the situation in Jesus's death on the cross as *atonement*. Paul does not explain how this atoning sacrifice generates salvific grace for others, nor who can be saved by this grace, other than it is "effective through faith." As was

---

16. Roman Catholic Church, *Catechism*, § 1024.
17. Aquinas, *Summa Theologiae*, 1–2:113.5.
18. Benedict XII, *Benedictus Deus*.

the case with original sin, the specifics of atonement theology remain a matter of debate. How are we saved by baptism? Is baptism required for salvation? Who can receive baptism?

The Classical Views of Anselm and Aquinas

Anselm of Canterbury addressed this question in 1089 AD in his treatise *Cur Deus Homo* or *Why God Became a Man*. Anselm theorized that human sin had broken off our relationship with God and left us so diminished that we could not make right what we had made wrong. God therefore reconciles us through the life and death of his only son, Jesus. Anselm saw the problem of original sin as that humanity was created to enjoy ultimate happiness, which, because of our sin, would be impossible unless our sins could be forgiven (1:10).[19] God created us for a better destiny than we are currently experiencing. This destiny is glimpsed in moments of fleeting happiness, but the fullness of happiness, which is our destiny, is beyond any of the joys we can experience here (1:24). Sin is placing our own will above God's will (1:11). Through doing this, we wrong God by disrupting God's plan for the world. To right this wrong we need to begin submitting our will to God's will, but in justice we also need to pay satisfaction—to do something to repair the damage that was caused by our disruption of God's plan (1:23).[20]

Here we run into a problem. Since God is the creator of the universe and everything in it, everything already belongs to God (1:20). There is nothing more that we can give to show our honor for God. We owe God our complete obedience, and we should act everywhere and always in

---

19. Anselm, *Cur Deus Homo*, 1:chap. 10. The rest of the references to Anselm will be given parenthetically in the text citing book number and chapter.

20. Eleonore Stump offers this helpful example of satisfaction: Young Nathan carelessly plays soccer near his mother Anna's prized flower garden, as he has been asked not to do, and ends up trampling her flowers. Anna has ruined flowers, but more importantly, the incident creates distance between herself and her son Nathan. Nathan cannot repair the flowers; he is too young. If he gives her only a half-hearted apology and continues to play soccer, he obviously does not love the flowers as his mom does, nor does he love his mother enough to care that he hurt her. If Nathan asked his older brother Aaron to help him fix the flowers, that would offer satisfaction, showing his love. If Aaron, by his own initiative, decided to repair the flower bed, Nathan could offer satisfaction by at least joining in the work as he could, thus showing that he wanted to help make things right. It is this last scenario that is most analogous to what Christ (as Aaron in the story) did for us (Stump, "Atonement According to Aquinas," 65–67).

conformity to God's will, so to offer to begin to obey God "more closely" is nothing more than what God is already due. There is nothing extra that we could do or give to make up for the damage we have caused by subverting God's will and we could not be truly happy in heaven without paying satisfaction for the hurt we have caused (1:24).

God solved this dilemma through the incarnation of his only son, Jesus, who is fully God and fully human (2:4). Jesus has something to offer God that we do not. As fully divine, Jesus could completely submit his will to the will of the Father (2:7). As fully human yet without sin, Jesus would not have had to die, so he has something to offer God that he does not already owe God—his human life. Jesus can offer satisfaction to God by allowing himself to be killed for the sake of following God's will, thus inspiring others to follow God more closely (2:18).

To explain, Anselm thought that if it was not for sin, people could live forever (2:11). For evidence he notes that Adam and Eve were immortal before the fall, yet were truly human, and we will be immortal in heaven, and yet still be truly human. Jesus was fully human yet without sin and so there would be no reason why he would have to die unless he freely chose to die. However, if he would allow himself to be killed for the sake of following God's will, Jesus could inspire others to follow God's will more diligently. This is something that Jesus could offer God to make up for God's plan being torn apart by humanity. Only someone who is fully divine would have the autonomous ability to lead a completely sinless life and since a human destroyed God's perfect plan, it is only fitting that someone who is fully human should pay the satisfaction. As Rachel Erdman explains this satisfaction, "Rather than compensating God, in the sense of making restitution to God for any damage our sin has caused God, Christ's satisfaction 'makes amends' by nullifying the evil of our sin. . . . In other words, it is not God who is satisfied in Anselm's scheme, but our *relationship* with God that was fractured by human sin."[21]

Jesus's sacrifice works both on the moral and ontological levels, repairing the damage done by sin both in the order of God's justice and in the human heart. In fact, it can only work on the ontological level as satisfaction for sin because it works on the moral level winning people over to follow God's will more closely. Because Jesus is fully human, we can identify and be inspired by him and the merit that he won can be given to us. For Anselm, the actions of Jesus could not save the devil,

---

21. Erdman, "Sacrifice as Satisfaction," 465.

"For, as man could not be reconciled but by the death of the God-man, by whose holiness the loss occasioned by man's sin should be made up; so fallen angels cannot be saved but by the death of a God-angel who by his holiness may repair the evil occasioned by the sins of his companions" (2:20). The savior would have to be the same species as those saved. All humanity is one species, and the medievals believed that each angel was a unique species, so there could never be a second angel of the same species to be an appropriate salvific figure.

Thomas Aquinas accepted Anselm's basic analysis but disagreed with him in some particulars, moving the discussion forward. Taking on the idea that the incarnate Son could have lived forever, Aquinas makes an important distinction. Agreeing that being sinless meant that Jesus would not have to die of necessity, Aquinas added that Jesus chose to take on our broken human condition, including death, in the act of becoming incarnate, and he justifies this with three reasons.[22] First, Jesus came to redeem our broken human condition, so it is fitting for him to take it on as it is, with its brokenness of which death is a part. Second, being familiar only with broken human nature, if he would have been incarnated with a perfect human nature such as we had in the Garden of Eden or will have in heaven, humanity would not have believed that he was truly human. Third, Jesus offers a better example of patience by taking on our broken human nature and bearing the ills that plague everyone. For these reasons, there would be no actual incarnate Son who could live forever, yet Jesus still freely chose to die. Jesus just made the choice to die in his heavenly preexistence when he chose to live as one of us.

Anselm had written that God could not simply forgive the debt we owed by fiat because we were unable to pay it since it would be unjust, and we could not be fully happy in heaven knowing that the debt was never paid. Aquinas extended this analysis as well, noting that God could be just in forgiving the debt since God is the one sinned against.[23] However, God's mercy is beyond human mercy and beyond human understanding. In responding to our sin, God went beyond healing it, forgiving the debt as it were, and used it as an opportunity to give us more than we had in the first place. There could not be a divine action that was merciful and unjust. Such an action would not actually be merciful at all. Not only is there no contradiction in God, all good things come together as one in the perfection of

---

22. Aquinas, *Summa Theologiae*, 3:14.2.
23. Aquinas, *Summa Theologiae*, 3:46.2 resp. 3.

God. Mercy that is unjust would have to be a false mercy. Saving humanity through the Incarnation was actually more merciful and more just than simply forgiving us without requiring satisfaction.[24] In God's superabundant mercy, the Incarnation does for us what was impossible before the fall—it allows us to enter into a more complete union with God in heaven. This grace is beyond our nature, even our perfected nature.[25] Our life with God in heaven is better than our life in the Garden of Eden. In the end, then, because of God's generous response in giving us Jesus Christ, humanity is better off because of the fall.

Anselm believed that Jesus, as God-man, could only save humans because his merit could only be given to other humans, the direct descendants of Adam and thus of the same species as Adam. Aquinas theorized more about why the merit gained by Jesus would be applied to other humans, thus giving an insight into which humans would be saved. Paul's Letter to the Romans quoted above indicates that faith is the essential condition for salvation. The Letter of Jas 2:26 adds that faith without works is dead, not implying that our actions save us, but that faith is not just what one thinks, but is a rich concept that has tangible manifestations in our life. In the Gospel of John 3:5, Jesus tells Nicodemus that no one can enter the kingdom of God without being born of water and Spirit. This has traditionally been interpreted as indicating the need to be baptized in order to be saved, though it is short of an absolute requirement for the sacrament of baptism. Two traditional examples of people who could be saved without receiving the sacrament of baptism are those who are martyred for the faith without receiving baptism, and those who die while preparing to receive baptism.[26] These are called the *baptism of blood* and the *baptism of desire* respectively. Still, receiving the actual sacrament of baptism is the ordinary and surest way to open the gates of heaven.

---

24. In his *Commentary on the Sentences of Peter Lombard*, an early work, Aquinas poses Boso's objection based on mercy thus: "It would have been more fitting for God to show the greatness of his mercy than the severity of his justice. Mercy dictates forgiveness of sins without satisfaction. Thus God could have saved man without assuming a human nature and even have wrought greater praise from mankind since he manifested greater mercy" (from 3:1.1.2 as found in Cessario, *Christian Satisfaction*, 73). Romanus Cessario explains that "it manifests [God's] mercy because the Incarnation is a greater demonstration of mercy, given all that it entails concerning the kenosis of the Word, than would have been the case had God chosen to absolve man without the satisfaction of the God-man" (Cessario, *Christian Satisfaction*, 77).

25. Aquinas, *Summa Theologiae*, 1–2:5.5 and 1–2:109.5.

26. Roman Catholic Church, *Catechism*, § 1258.

Thomas Aquinas believed that God did not randomly choose those to whom he distributed the merit won by Jesus, but that there was a real connection between Jesus and those who received this merit. Christ's passion causes the forgiveness of sins three ways.[27] The first way involves our wills: by enduring death the way he did, Jesus gave us an example of love (charity) that strengthens our own ability to love. The other two ways involved Jesus's human and divine natures. Through Jesus's human nature he was accessible to humans and through his divine nature his actions had salvific power. Since Jesus was human, we could be joined with him and share in his merit, "as if, by performing some meritorious work with his hands, a man might redeem himself from a sin he had committed with his feet." Because Jesus was incarnate he could be encountered, but to share in his merit we would also need to be joined with him as a member of his mystical body, the church. Aquinas concluded that those were forgiven their sins "provided we share in his passion by faith, love, and the sacraments of faith."[28] Faith and charity sprang from believing Jesus and following his ways, but it was through the sacraments of faith that we were actually joined to Jesus's mystical body and so had a real connection to him and the salvation he won for us.

By "sacraments of faith" Aquinas was referring primarily to the seven sacraments of the Catholic Church, and particularly to the sacrament of baptism by which we are joined to Christ by becoming a member of his mystical body, the church. But in addition to the "baptism of water" Aquinas affirmed the efficacy of the baptisms of blood and repentance similar to those noted above. One could be joined to Christ's passion without a baptism of water by either suffering for the sake of Christ—a baptism of blood—or by believing in and loving God and repenting of one's sins—a baptism of repentance.[29] Noting Paul's insistence on faith, however, Aquinas held that one of these means was required for salvation, so children who died before the age of reason and without the sacrament of baptism could not be saved by the work of Christ.[30]

---

27. Aquinas, *Summa Theologiae*, 3:49.1.

28. Aquinas, *Summa Theologiae*, 3:49.5. "Passion" refers to the suffering and death of Jesus on the cross.

29. Aquinas, *Summa Theologiae*, 3:66.11.

30. Aquinas, *Summa Theologiae*, 3:52.7.

Aquinas also taught that the necessity of the incarnation for our sake was not absolute, as food was absolutely necessary for life.[31] Instead, the incarnation of God was necessary for our salvation as a horse is necessary for a journey. It is "better and more expeditious." God, with omnipotent power, could have saved us other ways. God chose to save us through the incarnation.

Twentieth Century Catholic Expansion of the Scope of Salvation Explicitly Including Non-Christians

In the twentieth century the Roman Catholic Church continued to rethink the limits of the salvation won by Christ with a renewed emphasis on the belief that God wanted all people to be saved.[32] The 1994 *Catechism of the Catholic Church* states, "God has bound salvation to the sacrament of baptism, but he himself is not bound by his sacraments."[33] One interpretation of the meaning of this assertion is that the baptism of blood in martyrdom and the baptism of desire, neither of which are the sacrament of baptism, shows that God can save people outside of the strict limits of the sacrament. But in its context, more is asserted. Four paragraphs later the *Catechism* states, "Indeed, the great mercy of God who desires that all men should be saved, and Jesus's tenderness toward children which caused him to say: 'Let the children come to me, do not hinder them,' allow us to hope that there is a way of salvation for children who have died without baptism." Aquinas argued against this position and the *Catechism* gives no explanation about how this could be possible, but if we hope that children can be saved, surely God hopes for it even more, and has ways to accomplish goals that we cannot even fathom.

A larger movement came at the Second Vatican Council. The council's 1964 dogmatic constitution on the church, *Lumen Gentium*, placed the church at the center of a series of concentric circles of God's grace.[34] First, it noted that non-Catholic Christians are linked to the church through their baptism, and the document speaks of hope for unity among all Christians. It then moves on to consider non-Christians, starting with the Jewish people, affirming along with Paul's Letter to the Romans that God's gifts and calling

---

31. Aquinas, *Summa Theologiae*, 3:1.2.
32. As asserted in 1 Tim 2:4.
33. Roman Catholic Church, *Catechism*, § 1257.
34. Roman Catholic Church, *Lumen Gentium*, § 15–16.

to them are irrevocable. Widening the circle further, *Lumen Gentium* notes that Muslims believe in the same God as do Christians and are included in God's plan of salvation. It then notes that those who through no fault of their own simply have a vague notion of an unknown God, can be saved by trying to please this unknown God by following the dictates of their conscience. Lastly, it makes the broad assertion that, "Nor does Divine Providence deny the helps necessary for salvation to those who, without blame on their part, have not yet arrived at an explicit knowledge of God and with his grace strive to live a good life. Whatever good or truth is found amongst them is looked upon by the church as a preparation for the Gospel." God can save even those who do not believe in him because he is working in the world outside the boundaries of the church. As it is written in *Gaudium et Spes*, a later document of the Council, "Since Christ died for all men, and since the ultimate vocation of man is in fact one, and divine, we ought to believe that the Holy Spirit in a manner known only to God offers to every man the possibility of being associated with this paschal mystery."[35]

The quote is not intended to be gender-exclusive; Christ died to save all people regardless of gender. The text affirms that *we ought to believe* that God offers salvation to all people, even non-Christians, through associating them with the salvific work of Jesus Christ. One does not have to be a Christian or even explicitly know about Christ to be saved in Christ. Salvation is not exclusive to Christians, even though it comes exclusively through Christ.

Christianity takes history seriously, and there is an inherent tension that arises from connecting universal salvation to a particular person who lived at a particular time and place. What about those who lived elsewhere or at a different time? Imagine the plight of a good and pious woman who prayed and sought to do the will of God as she understood it but was born in the second century on an island that now comprises part of New Zealand. This Maori maiden would have lived her life with no chance of hearing anything about the revelation of Jesus of Nazareth. Her island was physically isolated from the Middle East and there is no indication that trade and exchange of ideas was possible in the second century. Are we to believe that any prayers of hers to *an unknown God* went completely unheard or unheeded? Was God powerless to respond? Or did God make an active decision against this woman by choosing to send Jesus where and when he did, cutting off her access to him? Even if news of Jesus Christ

---

35. Roman Catholic Church, *Gaudium et Spes*, § 22.

reached her island a few centuries later, giving the Maori a chance to believe in Jesus, it would not have helped her or anyone who lived and died in her generation. Instead of believing her to be an unfortunate casualty of history, geographically cut off from salvation, *Gaudium et Spes* proposes that it is better to believe that God has ways to save her that we do not understand. Salvation still comes through Christ, but not in any way that we can trace historically. *Gaudium et Spes* would have us believe that salvation in Christ does not necessarily require any physical connection or traceable transmission of information from Jesus of Nazareth through his apostles to the individual being saved.

Speculative Twenty-First Century Expansion of the Scope of Salvation including Non-humans

Where is the boundary beyond which salvation in Jesus Christ is not possible? Is salvation in Christ exclusive to *Homo sapiens*? In his encyclical *Laudato Si*, Pope Francis opened up this question by referencing the Letter to the Colossians, asserting: "In the Christian understanding of the world, the destiny of all creation is bound up with the mystery of Christ, present from the beginning: 'All things have been created through him and for him.'"[36] Francis teaches that there is a place in heaven for everything in creation, and that every creature has something unique to offer the people who have been resurrected:

> At the end, we will find ourselves face to face with the infinite beauty of God, and be able to read with admiration and happiness the mystery of the universe, which with us will share in unending plenitude. Even now we are journeying towards the sabbath of eternity, the new Jerusalem, towards our common home in heaven. Jesus says: "I make all things new." Eternal life will be a shared experience of awe, in which each creature, resplendently transfigured, will take its rightful place and have something to give those poor men and women who will have been liberated once and for all.[37]

In Francis's view, Jesus was constantly in touch with nature, reminding people of God's paternal love for all creatures with his parables: "With moving tenderness he would remind them that each one of them is important

36. Francis, *Laudato Si*, § 99.
37. Francis, *Laudato Si*, § 243.

in God's eyes: 'Are not five sparrows sold for two pennies? And not one of them is forgotten before God.'"[38] We might not value all creatures, but God does, so we might justly hope that our pets might be with us in heaven. And if dogs and cats, why not warthogs? It seems so, and it would be good to ponder the beauty of resplendently transfigured warthog bodies. But if God loves *all* creatures, what about those that live on other planets? What about the possibility of salvation for sentient beings that developed on other planets and had free will and could understand truth and could love? In the following, we will designate them poetically as "Martians." At this point we know that there is not sentient life on Mars. There might still be some kind of life, but not sentient species like *Homo sapiens*. So "Martians" can be used metaphorically and somewhat picturesquely to designate intelligent life that originated on a planet other than Earth.

Considering the salvation of Martians requires pondering a series of related questions: 1) Are there Martians? 2) If so, would Martians stand in need of salvation? 3) If so, could Martians be saved by the work of Jesus Christ, the God-human, or would they require, for instance, a God-Martian? 4) If Martians could be saved by the work of Jesus, would God save them this way, or would God devise some other means to save them?

1. Are There Martians?

To begin, we do not know if there are Martians. There could be. The universe is a very large place, and it is possible that life could have evolved on another planet in isolation from life on Earth. This life could have become sentient over time, just as we have. We have no indication that this has happened, nor do we have disconfirmation. There are various mathematical analyses of the probability of such life, but they are inconclusive.[39]

Lutheran theologian Ted Peters has advocated for the modern Christian community to think more deeply about the theological significance of extraterrestrial intelligence.[40] He has shown that there is a long history of thought on the subject, from the ancient Greeks through medieval Christians, including Thomas Aquinas, who held that "the very order of things created by God shows the unity of the world."[41] Peters sums up Aquinas's

---

38. Francis, *Laudato Si*, § 96.
39. For an interesting survey of various positions on this issue see Al-Khalili, *Aliens*.
40. Peters, "Exotheology," 121–22.
41. Aquinas, *Summa Theologiae*, 1:47.3.

position thus: "He agrees with Aristotle that our world is ordered, not by chance as Democritus and the atomists said, but by the principle of unity tending toward perfection. Be that as it may, the Thomistic view is definitely in favor of one world, not many."[42] By this, Peters means that Aquinas favors the view that life existed on only one planet, not many planets. However, the word Aquinas uses for world, *mundus*, is also the word one uses for the universe or all of creation. By the logic of Aquinas's argument, all of created reality is one since it all comes under the one plan of God. The argument would be equally applicable if there were multiple inhabited planets in the universe or even if there were a multiverse. Peters went on to contrast Aquinas's position with the views of other medieval theologians, noting that Nicole Oresme (1320–1382) argued in favor of the possibility of multiple worlds, each with its own center, adding that Oresme's view "denies the position of both Aristotle and Thomas that all things in the same universe must have a relation to one another." But Oresme's view is not contrary to Aquinas's. All things in the universe have a relationship to one another by virtue of being in the same universe, and they are all related in God's overarching plan of creation. They would not cease to have this unity if there were multiple centers of attraction, with some things attracted to one center and other things attracted to another center, just as humanity does not cease to have a unity just because some people call one place home and others call another place home.

2. Would Martians Need Salvation?

If Martians exist, Pinker points out that they are probably the product of natural selection, since "natural selection is the only explanation we have of how complex life *can* evolve."[43] The process of natural selection slowly evolves breeding populations over time, with the next iteration being better than the last in some reproductive or life-sustaining way. But natural selection never produces perfection. That would be quite improbable, given that it is based on random mutations. Consequently, Martians would most likely be in a state of original sin, as are we, plagued by conflicting desires and incapable of consistently making perfect decisions.[44] If Martians were

---

42. Peters, "Exotheology," 123.

43. Pinker, *How the Mind Works*, 155. Pinker credits the original insight to Richard Dawkins.

44. Note that this is at odds with the popular religious science-fiction book *Perelandra*,

in the state of original sin, it seems that our loving God would offer them a way out just as God did for Earthlings.

From a theological standpoint we could also note that Aquinas taught that humanity's ability to know and to love showed that its ultimate destiny was to know and love God directly, a destiny that is beyond our nature, even our perfected nature. It is only through the grace that comes through Christ Jesus that we are able to achieve our ultimate destiny. By this logic, the ultimate destiny of Martians, who can know and love, would be the same—to know and to love God in heaven.[45] The genetic similarity of all *Homo sapiens* gives each one a free will and a potentiality for knowledge and love. These are the things that allow us to fully live out God's plan for the world—to know God, to love God, and to serve God. But if Martians were truly sentient and had free will and the ability to know and to love—even if these abilities were based in other genetic configurations, or other chemical processes, such as silicon-based chemistry—they would be able to fully live out God's plan for the world just as we would. They would have a place beside us in heaven.

They would also be able to join with us in bringing about God's plan for the universe here and now, and so they should be welcomed to become part of the church, the body of Christ. The aggregation to the church is spiritual, not physical, and to believe that it would be impossible for a physical and spiritual being because of a different genetic makeup seems odd.

Neither getting to heaven nor becoming part of the church is naturally possible for a physical being without the addition of God's grace, regardless of the person's status *vis-a-vis* original sin. Thus, we are compelled to believe that God would offer all physical, sentient beings this grace.

Buddhism has similar insights that offer helpful comparisons. Symbolized in the six realms that appear in paintings of the *Wheel of Life*, Buddhism teaches that mind-streams pass through a series of incarnations, only some of which are human.[46] The six realms of existence—divine, semi-divine, human, animal, hungry ghost, and hell—speak of the variety of

---

the second volume of C. S. Lewis's space trilogy, which is premised on the idea that Venus houses a separate original couple, essentially a Venetian Adam and Eve, still living in their own Garden of Eden. Our hero, Elwin Ransom, tries to preserve them from falling into sin as did his race.

45. As Aquinas says, "God is the ultimate end of all things without exception.... Men and other rational creatures lay hold of it in knowing and loving God" (Aquinas, *Summa Theologiae*, 1–2:1.8).

46. Explained in the second chapter, pp. 29–30.

possibilities for sentient life. These realms are not identical but they are all equally part of the wheel of life, and mind-streams typically pass through many of them on their way to enlightenment.

A further refinement of Mahayana Buddhism addressed the issue of how it was possible for a finite mind to become enlightened, since a finite mind is limited and the enlightened buddha-mind is unbounded, with infinite awareness. It is logically impossible for something finite to grow into something infinite. Thus, the infinite buddha-nature must already exist inside sentient beings, albeit in a hidden way. Religious practice does not need to create an enlightened, unbounded mind; it only needs to free it. The buddha-nature within each sentient being is called the *tathagatagarbha*. The oldest scripture on the tathagatagarbha, the third century *Tathagatagarbha Sutra*, offers nine metaphors to help picture this, such as gold that has fallen unnoticed into a pit of waste.[47] It does not decay and remains worth a fortune, but no one knows it is there until someone comes along with supernatural vision, sees it, and tells people to start digging. The fifth century *Uttaratantra Shastra* repeats the nine metaphors from the *Tathagatagarbha Sutra*, but adds another, more allegorical image as well: the tathagatagarbha is like the sky with the sun shining on a cloudy day.[48] You cannot see it, but you know that the sun is up there behind the clouds. To allow the sun to shine, you do not have to create the sun or the sky, you simply need to clear away the clouds. The clouds are like the defilements of *kleshas* built up by bad karma over eons. Buddhist practice works like an inexorable wind, clearing away the clouds.

There are differing views about what the tathagatagarbha consists of and whether or not it exists with qualities of clarity and luminosity inside each sentient being, but Tsongkhapa taught that the tathagatagarbha refers to the dependent existence at the core of each person.[49] Since there is nothing fixed about us, we have no inherent limitations and are completely unbounded at our core. Enlightenment allows one to experience and know this unboundedness. What is significant for our discussion here is that there can be no distinction between the tathagatagarbha in various sentient beings. Dependent existence at the core of every sentient being

---

47. Dating the text from Lopez, *Buddhism in Practice*, 92. Image of gold from Lopez, *Buddhism in Practice*, 98.

48. Dating of the text from Williams, *Mahayana Buddhism*, 103. Image of the clouds in the sky is found throughout, but is explained well in Gyamtso, *Buddha Nature*, 134, 184.

49. Tsongkhapa, *Great Treatise*, 3:198.

has to be the same, or it would be bounded and defined one way in one person and another way in another person. It does not matter whether tathagatagarbha is apparent and active in a particular mind-stream, it must still be there, unbounded and unchanged whether within a human, divine, or hungry ghost incarnation.

The Buddhist notion of tathagatagarbha can be productively compared with Pope Francis's vision of salvation of all creatures. Tathagatagarbha is like salvific grace in that both are an infinite reality operative at the core of individuals that allows for them to transcend all boundaries—for the Buddhist enabling enlightenment, and for the Christian enabling life with God in heaven. Both concepts emphasize the inherent value of living creatures, or at least all sentient ones. These ideas are dissimilar in that the tathagatagarbha is thought to be an inherent part of every sentient being while salvific grace is thought to originate outside the individual and is given by God.[50]

Historically and biblically, Christians have envisioned multitudes of different kinds of creatures besides just humans with God in heaven—cherubim and seraphim, angels, powers, thrones, etc. If these created realities can exist with God in heaven, why would we think resurrected Martians could not? Since God created the universe to share in the joy of the divine life, wouldn't anything that could share in that joy find a home in heaven where the fullness of joy resides? Would Martians have their own heaven or their own path to heaven, segregated from Earthlings? This also seems odd. Since life in heaven is not natural to any biological creature, any biological sentient creature would stand in need of salvation to find its ultimate fulfillment, and it seems that God would want to have all such creatures in heaven.

3. Could Jesus Save Martians?

Which leads to the next question, how to give such creatures the grace to get to heaven? Could it come through the grace won by Jesus Christ, or would God have to find a different avenue of grace, perhaps creating a different divine incarnation? The grace won by Christ is sufficient to redeem the

---

50. The argument that tathagatagarbha must be alike in all creatures is strikingly similar to one of Aquinas's arguments that God must be one: if there were two unlimited beings, whatever distinguished them would be a limitation, which is contradictory. See Aquinas, *Summa Theologiae*, 1:11.3.

entire universe, so we cannot think that it is lacking in power. But Anselm raised a different concern. According to Anselm's logic, different species would require different saviors—Jesus, the God-human to save humans and perhaps Zorkon, the God-Martian to save Martians.

As the second person of the Trinity, Jesus is uncreated, begotten not made, one in being with God from before the beginning of time. But Jesus's human nature has not always existed. It was created in time and has existence by being united to the second person of the Trinity. It is conceivable that God could create a Martian nature, uniting it to the second person of the Trinity so that Jesus now had a second incarnation. Such is the theological opinion of noted twentieth-century Jesuit theologian Karl Rahner, who wrote:

> In view of the immutability of God in himself and the identity of the Logos with God, it cannot be proved that a multiple incarnation in different histories of salvation is absolutely unthinkable. . . . Theology need not put any absolute veto on the idea of history of spirit on another star. Theologians will not be able to say anything further on this question. They will point to the fact that the purpose of Christian revelation is the salvation of humankind, not to provide an answer to questions which really have no important bearing on the realization of this salvation in freedom.[51]

Rahner posits that Christianity is for earthlings only. He notes that while it is our belief that salvation comes from God through the second person of the Trinity, there is no theological necessity that would bar another incarnation on another planet. In that case, Jesus would be the unique savior of earthlings, but the other incarnation would be the unique savior of beings on that other planet. Rahner is correct about the theological possibility of multiple incarnations, but he is not correct that nothing more can be said.

It is certainly not obvious that Christianity is for earthlings only. In the biblical record the angels line up to see Jesus's birth, and the Letter to the Philippians proclaims: "at the name of Jesus every knee should bend, in heaven and on earth and under the earth, and every tongue should confess that Jesus Christ is Lord, to the glory of God the Father" (Phil 2:10–11, NRSV). This is Jesus, the incarnate son of God, not simply the *Logos*, the second person of the Trinity. In Rahner's favor there is Anselm's objection:

---

51. Rahner, *Science and Christian Faith*, 51–52. The page numbers refer to the pagination in the German original. It is worth noting that the first part of the assertion, the *possibility* of multiple incarnations of the second person of the Trinity, is also accepted by Aquinas in *Summa Theologiae*, 3:3.7.

can grace obtained by a human savior be given to non-humans? But this seems entirely possible for God, who made all things, human and non-human alike. In a classical worldview, all humans were bound together by partaking in a single human nature. In a worldview informed by modern theories of evolution, human nature is no longer so neat a category. What constitutes a species is rather malleable, with fuzzy edges. It is difficult to believe that Jesus would only have a connection to life forms with a nearly identical genetic makeup. After all, couldn't Martians be inspired by the life of Jesus and see themselves reflected in his story? Couldn't we earthlings be inspired by the story of Zorkon and see our own struggles reflected in that story, or would we simply see it as alien and not applicable to us? These stories of salvation seem universal and universally accessible.

As Aquinas noted, the ultimate destiny of any creature that can know and love is to know and love God in heaven. This is just as true for Martians as it is for humans. Beyond this, imagine human Christians one day finally meeting Martians. Would they withhold telling them about the Good News in Jesus Christ because he was *our* savior and not *theirs*? Is the Gospel not *Good News* for Martians? Surely, if they were Martians of good will, Christians would want to work with them to help bring about better lives for all. If, in seeing our motivation, a Martian wanted to convert to Christianity, to follow in the footsteps of Jesus, would we say no, that was impossible? On what basis would we deny them? Would it really be impossible for God to make them part of the church, God who made the universe and everything in it, and sent his Son to redeem it? This is where Rahner is wrong in stating that this issue has no bearing on the realization of salvation here on Earth. Do we really think the Good News in Jesus Christ is so small?

Becoming a member of the church, aggregated to the body of Christ, surely does not rely on our genetic makeup. It is a work of the Holy Spirit, a miracle wrought by grace, which transforms our spiritual-physical natures. Perhaps a purely spiritual being such as an angel could not be a part of the church on earth, which exists in the world, but why would we think it would be impossible for a Martian? This seems like spiritual racism.

4. Would God Save Martians Some Other Way?

One could argue that it would be more expedient for God to send a different savior to a planet 100 million light years from Earth, since it would be a long time before the saving message of Jesus of Nazareth could get there.

In this vast universe, there is room and need for many incarnations. Such is the opinion of Thomas O'Meara, who writes eloquently of the love of God seeking to reach out in a myriad of ways:

> The divine motive for fashioning a universe of galaxies is God's goodness; the same motive brings incarnation. As incarnation is an intense form of divine love, would there not be galactic forms of that love? An infinite being of generosity would tend to many incarnations rather than to one. The inner life of divine self surging out of three divine persons suggests multiple incarnations; reflection on the dynamics of Trinity and incarnation leads to community activity, not to isolation. A succession of incarnations would give new relationships and new self-realizations to God.[52]

This is a beautiful vision of the love of God reaching out through all of creation. O'Meara, in his extended treatment of the subject, also deals with some objections. Further incarnations would not compete with each other but extend the revelation of God, since "the man Jesus of Nazareth remains minute compared to the Word of God."[53] God is not limited by the incarnation and is free to act in an infinite number of ways to save creation.

But this vision is problematic in another way. Consider the second-century Maori maiden mentioned earlier. The Second Vatican Council urged us to believe that her salvation could be achieved through the incarnation of Jesus and the paschal mystery even though she had no possible historical connection to Jesus of Nazareth.[54] The barriers of time and space that separated her from the historical Jesus and his message are not barriers for God's grace won through Christ in his incarnation. If this is true, then barriers of time and space between present day Earth and extraterrestrial sentient beings would also be no barrier for God's grace. The difference between bridging an ocean and the vast vacuum of space is nothing for God. The important step is to believe that grace can be given without a historical connection.

Wouldn't this Maori maiden be justified in complaining at the pearly gates of heaven if she got there and found out that the Martians got their own savior while her people did not? Many generations of her people lived and died with no access to the saving words of Jesus of Nazareth because they were simply too far away from the event, which had happened

---

52. O'Meara, *Vast Universe*, 47.
53. O'Meara, *Vast Universe*, 48.
54. Roman Catholic Church, *Lumen Gentium*, § 16.

in a distant culture. O'Meara notes that a further incarnation "is also a dramatic mode of showing love for and identification with that race," and "incarnations would correspond to the forms of intelligent creature with their own religious quests."[55] Did God not love the Maori enough to become incarnate there? Was the second-century Maori religious quest not worth entering into?

The religious quest of the Maori in second century Earth was separate from that of Jewish Christians of the same period. If we are to suppose that God loves all creatures and reaches out to them all, then we cannot think that the only way this can happen is through an historical connection to their own incarnation, which many cultures on Earth did not have. There would be too many people left out, with no hope of connection to God's saving Word. If we are to believe that God identifies with each race, this identification cannot be done solely through becoming incarnate in each. We do not need to look to the stars to see this. Second century Maori were cut off from access to the words of Jesus Christ and had no incarnation of their own.[56] Does that mean that God and the Word of God was not present to them? Not if God loved them; not if the words of *Gaudium et Spes* are true, that God offers salvation to *everyone*.

The solution lies in taking seriously the words of *Lumen Gentium*: that whatever good or truth is found amongst beings of other places and time, who do not have sufficient access to the fullness of revelation that comes through the incarnation in Jesus of Nazareth, is looked upon by the church as a preparation for the Gospel. God loves them enough to have not left them completely bereft. God has been planting seeds of truth with them that are sufficient for their salvation. To believe that if God did not show up in their culture with the fullness of an incarnation then God did not show up, or did not love them, or did not do enough to allow them to enter into the fullness of life in heaven, is to believe in a very small God, one who did not love the Maori. This is not the God of Jesus Christ.

---

55. O'Meara, *Vast Universe*, 48.

56. Some theologians have used this line of reasoning to argue that the founders of other religions here on Earth could be thought of as alternative incarnations of God in some sense, and thus as salvific for their communities, but the Roman Catholic Church has resisted this. For instance, the Congregation for the Doctrine of the Faith has asserted: "The theory which would attribute, after the incarnation as well, a salvific activity to the Logos as such in his divinity, exercised 'in addition to' or 'beyond' the humanity of Christ, is not compatible with the Catholic faith" (Roman Catholic Church, *Dominus Iesus*, § 10).

O'Meara is correct is pointing to the dynamism of the Trinity and the love of God leading us to believe that God is constantly reaching out to all cultures. But God has more ways than one to reach people. God could become incarnate again, but our own history leads us to believe that instead God reaches out in every time and place and culture in diverse ways, and uses the one incarnation as the center of salvific activity around which the rest turns. If incarnations were a common thing, then we would have expected God to have sent one to every culture, including the second-century Maori. If there is only one incarnation, then it had to be somewhere, rooted in one place and time, excluding other places and other times. This is the nature of what it means to be incarnated. If there is only a single incarnation we would expect God to find other ways to be present in every culture, and this is what *Gaudium et Spes* encourages us to believe. In this light, the Holy Spirit could have worked through the Buddha to place whatever good or truth is found amongst Buddhists, and this would be seen as a preparation for the Gospel of Jesus Christ, not as an alternative to it. If Buddhists are saved, they are saved by Jesus Christ, even if they do not know him.[57] But when Christians preach the Good News to Buddhists, they should not proceed as if God had never been there before—they should look for seeds of the word and signs of God's work and build upon them. If some day human Christians meet Martians, they should do the same. To believe that God sends separate incarnations to extraterrestrial cultures throughout the universe but not an ocean away from Jesus is akin to offering more kindness to strangers than to one's own family. It is possible, but it seems wrong.

Conclusions

The question of extraterrestrial salvation is not merely an intellectual exercise; it has real implications about how we think about those in our own world that were excluded from a meaningful historical connection to Jesus Christ. *Lumen Gentium,* the *Dogmatic Constitution of the Church* begins:

> Christ is the Light of nations. Because this is so, this Sacred Synod gathered together in the Holy Spirit eagerly desires, by proclaiming the Gospel to every creature, to bring the light of Christ to all

---

57. In the same way, Isa 45 claims that the God of Israel was leading the Persian king Cyrus in battle, proclaiming, "I arm you, though you do not know me, so that they may know, from the rising of the sun and from the west, that there is no one besides me" (NRSV).

> men, a light brightly visible on the countenance of the Church. Since the Church is in Christ like a sacrament or as a sign and instrument both of a very closely knit union with God and of the unity of the whole human race, it desires now to unfold more fully to the faithful of the Church and to the whole world its own inner nature and universal mission.[58]

This is a beautiful, prophetic statement about the purview of God's plan and the role of the church in helping to bring it about. Can we imagine that Christ is the Light not just of the nations on Earth, but also of the entire universe? Can we imagine preaching the Gospel to every creature, not simply to other *Homo sapiens*? What would happen if we encountered intelligent life forms that developed on other planets? Would we proclaim to them the Good News of Jesus Christ, or would we keep that to ourselves as a revelation "for earthlings only"? Just how universal do we see the mission of the church? Could we envision the church one day being a sign of the unity not just of the human race but of all sentient beings, or do we believe that this is a division too large for Jesus Christ to bridge?

It seems justified to believe that all manner of creatures will be saved in Christ, and to not look for another dispensation to save extraterrestrial beings should they exist. Such belief is not far from the Catholic imagination as manifested in the array of beings pictured surrounding the heavenly throne of God in Baroque churches. It is in line with the cosmic view of God's plan found in the Letter to the Ephesians which says, "With all wisdom and insight [God] has made known to us the mystery of his will, according to his good pleasure that he set forth in Christ, as a plan for the fullness of time, to gather up all things in him, things in heaven and things on earth" (Eph 1:8–10, NRSV). This passage looks beyond the unity of all people and puts forth a vision that in the end, the entire universe will be one in Christ.

A Vision of Heaven

As a final area of investigation, let us see if Christians might want to reimagine heaven through contrasting Christian views with those of Buddhism and naturalism. As explained in the previous chapter, both naturalism and Buddhism portray the existence of a soul as an illusion that needs to be

---

58. Roman Catholic Church, *Lumen Gentium*, § 1.

seen through if we are to understand the truth about the world.[59] Without a soul, Christians believe there is nothing about an individual that can exist forever. For naturalism, the beginning and the end of the life of an individual is rather fuzzy, with somewhat arbitrary boundaries between living and not living, but in the end, nothing remains of the individual other than memories and the physical remnants that we can see and measure. For Tsongkhapa, what is unique to any mind-stream is ultimately delusion that needs to be purified.[60] This is why ultimately the individual does not exist. The tathagatagarbha, which is the buddha-nature at the core of every sentient being that allows for enlightenment, is common to all sentient beings, so ultimately, while individuals function as individuals in this dependent world of illusion, nothing of the individual exists ultimately, able to survive forever in some putative ultimate heaven.

In contrast, Christianity claims that God makes individual souls for each human person, and that God therefore loves individuals and wants to save them in their individuality.[61] This salvation involves a physical resurrection, and Christians believe that we will have bodies in heaven.[62] Christians have staunchly defended the reality of physical resurrection against both a belief that there is nothing after this life and a belief in a merely mental resurrection, and the difference between physical and non-physical resurrection should be evident in the experience of those in heaven.

Aquinas had some controversial ideas about heaven that were vehemently opposed by other theologians in his day—even a pope—though his position eventually was definitively accepted as Catholic doctrine in 1336 by Pope Benedict XII in his constitution on the beatific vision, *Benedictus Deus*.[63] Aquinas proposed that when the just die they are immediately rewarded with the experience of the beatific vision, even before their bodies rise.[64] As separated souls they have a direct experience of God. It is natural for souls to be united to bodies and for people to experience reality through their bodies, so eventually there will come a general resurrection when God

---

59. For Buddhism, see pp. 40–41. For naturalism, see pp. 58–59.

60. See pp. 40–42.

61. Roman Catholic Church, *Catechism*, § 366.

62. Paul argues for physical resurrection in 1 Cor 15.

63. For an explanation of the controversy and its import, see Bynum, *Resurrection of the Body*, 229–78.

64. Aquinas, *Summa Theologiae*, 1–2:4.5. Also asserted in Aquinas, *Summa Contra Gentiles*, 4:91.10.

will resurrect our bodies and reunite them with our souls so that the just can experience the beatific vision through their bodies as well. After the resurrection, the just can experience the beatific vision more completely by using their senses, and "all are agreed that there is some sensation in the bodies of the blessed: else the bodily life of the saints after the resurrection would be likened to sleep rather than to vigilance."[65]

Some argue that Aquinas is against the view that there is time in heaven since he sees our greatest beatitude as simply beholding God, an experience that is timeless by nature. After all, Aquinas will sometimes say that human fulfillment can only be found in "complete repose or changelessness."[66] However, though Aquinas does not comment on time directly, the sequence of existence as separated souls followed by bodily resurrection necessitates having time in heaven. Also, having sensations in our resurrected bodies necessitates having time in heaven. Sensations happen in time. Ideas can be argued to be timeless, but sensations are always tied to the physical world and time. To say you are having a particular sensation means that you did not have it a while ago (and it will probably go away in a bit). Otherwise you could not identify it as a particular sensation. The same is not true for ideas. In addition, if there were no experience of time in heaven yet there was an experience of physical location—which must be true if we have bodies and sensations—there would be no motion and the relationship between various things in heaven would be forever fixed. We would have a location and be forever closer to some things and farther from other things, never being able to draw near to them. This does not seem to be a part of anyone's view of heaven. To give up experiencing in heaven would be tantamount to giving up life in heaven, for what would life be without experience? To give up having a location in heaven would seem tantamount to giving up belief in a physical resurrection, because there would be no difference between physical and nonphysical resurrection. Lastly, what are Catholics asking when they ask Mary and the saints to pray for them, which is a common feature of their official liturgical prayer? If there were no time in heaven, the saints could not pray for us or respond to our requests.

There is a significant difficulty in working out what Aquinas's mature position would have been on the question of time and progression in heaven because he did not finish the section of the *Summa Theologiae* that covers this question. The best material we have from Aquinas about

---

65. Aquinas, *Summa Theologiae*, Supplement:83.3.
66. Aquinas, *Compendium of Theology*, 1:149.

the resurrection is from the Supplement, which is an attempt by Aquinas's brothers to complete the *Summa Theologiae* after his death using his notes and earlier works. One tantalizing possibility is that he may have revised his view in something like the way he did with his view of Christ's human knowledge. These views are connected because Aquinas believed that Christ had the beatific vision—the heavenly vision of God—even in this life.[67] Nevertheless, in writing the *Summa* Aquinas claimed that there was a kind of development in Jesus's knowledge during his life, a view he had earlier denied. Although Aquinas thinks that Christ in his humanity knows all things, nevertheless the knowledge that Jesus has is made more explicit, spelled out more, as he gets older.[68] Aquinas explicitly addresses, in regard to us, that human knowing in heaven will still principally be through considering concepts one by one, that is, having a sequence that is at least time-like.[69] Perhaps, then, Aquinas could have believed that when we are in Heaven, we too will have the vision of God as a single act undergirding our whole heavenly lives, and nevertheless, our knowledge of God and his actions will grow and develop.

Time as the Fourth Dimension

Albert Einstein revolutionized science and ushered in modern physics through his general theory of relativity. Einstein sought to understand the reason for an anomaly in classical physics, that the speed of light in a vacuum was constant, irrespective of the motion of the observer.[70] This is something that is difficult to notice in our day-to-day experience, but with the advent of telescopes that could look at the stars and the planets, it became a problem that could not be explained. Imagine being on a train track with a locomotive coming at you at 100 miles per hour. You could measure its speed and see that it was coming at you at 100 miles per hour. You would probably be concerned. Now imagine that you were not just on the track, but were standing on a train on the same track that was also moving at 100 miles per hour in the same direction as the other train. You

---

67. Aquinas, *Summa Theologiae*, 3:9.2.

68. Aquinas, *Summa Theologiae*, 3:12.2.

69. Aquinas, *Sentences*, 1:1.4.2 resp. 2.

70. Einstein believed that his general and special theories of relativity were not beyond the understanding of the average educated person, and he wrote a popular work to explain them: Einstein, *Relativity*.

would be less concerned, because while you could measure your speed at 100 miles per hour, the other train would not be gaining on you. Its speed relative to yours would be zero. It would remain at the same distance from you. Now imagine that your train was moving in the opposite direction, toward the other train on the same track. The two trains would be coming together at 200 miles per hour, since you and it are both going 100 miles per hour toward each other. You would probably be quite concerned, perhaps even panicked.

Something unexpected happens, however, when we make these measurements at speeds that approach the speed of light. If a beam of light is coming toward us, rather than a cosmic train, it appears to be closing on us at a fixed speed whether we are going toward it or away from it. The speed of light is always the same, 671 million miles per hour. Unlike the train example, which makes perfect sense, our motion, relative to a beam of light, does not change the speed at which light appears to be approaching. Whether we are going toward it at 100 million miles per hour or going away from it at 100 million miles per hour, it appears to be coming at us at 671 million miles per hour.

Einstein theorized that this was possible if time and space were intrinsically related such that space was contracted in the direction of relative motion. The specifics of Einstein's theory relativity are difficult and there are a number of counterintuitive consequences, but they have proven to be quite accurate in explaining how the universe works. It appears, therefore, that Einstein's insight that time and space are intrinsically related is true.

While we speak of a three-dimensional world, we actually live in a four-dimensional world, with three physical dimensions and time as the fourth dimension. Steven Pinker has shown how the equivalence of time and space is even encoded into our language, as spatial metaphors for time appear in every language.[71] For instance, in English we might say, "That's all behind us," or "The time for action has arrived," or "We've passed the deadline," all of which rely on picturing time as having a physical location. The specific relationship between time and space varies, but we have no problem in understanding these metaphors, to the point of perhaps not even recognizing that they are metaphors.

Modern String Theory is exploring the possibility that the universe has even more than four dimensions, but this does not annul an intrinsic connection between time and space. To understand the implications of

---

71. Pinker, *Stuff of Thought*, 191–97.

multidimensional space, imagine Flatland, a universe with just two physical dimensions, like a piece of paper.[72] Not much would change. We could see each other and move past each other just as we do now, only in two dimensions instead of three. But then imagine that something existed in Flatland that could move in three dimensions. By moving in this additional dimension, it could move off the page, giving it the ability to disappear from one place on the paper and reappear in another, without having to travel from the first to the second. It could go through walls at will by going around them in the other dimension. Such are the possibilities that string theories explore. But any movement at all implies time, and thus Flatland would have three, not two total dimensions, two physical dimensions and time. Time is required for movement, and change, and life.

Quantum physics also opens up the possibility that the universe is actually far more complex than it appears to us on a conventional level, though in a different way. At the level where quantum physics comes into play, particles such as electrons cannot be pinned to a specific location at a specific time. Instead, they have a probability of being in certain places that is spread over space and time. Erwin Schrödinger theorized that these various probabilities were not simply alternatives but all really happen simultaneously in alternative universes.[73] Thus, perhaps there are an infinite number of universes that all exist simultaneously, and we only experience one of them.

In the two views just cited, additional dimensions and alternative universes are still related to the conventional world of our experience through the physical laws that govern the universe. Thus, heaven, as Christians think about it, could not be hiding in these additional dimensions or alternative universes. Though heaven is a place, it is not a part of or connected to this universe. However, our hypothesis is that if there is space in heaven at all, then there is time. We hypothesize that the intrinsic connection between time and space is not just true for this universe or for us in this life, but is simply *true*, so that it would also be true in heaven, which is not of this universe but has physical dimensions. Heaven must have physical dimensions or it would make no sense to proclaim a *bodily* resurrection—rather than a merely mental resurrection—as Christians do. But the physical dimensions

---

72. The idea of Flatland comes from a satirical novella by Edwin Abbott, *Flatland: A Romance of Many Dimensions*, published in 1884. However, the idea of this two-dimensional world helping us to understand multidimensional physics has taken on a life of its own. For a very good description, watch Sagan, "Flatland."

73. Gribbin, *Erwin Schrödinger*, 222.

in heaven do not correlate to the physical dimensions in this universe. Heaven is not up or down, above or below us, as we reckon these things. A physical heaven that made sense of a bodily resurrection would have dimensions, but they would be different dimensions corresponding to a different space. In the same way, if time is intrinsically linked to space, then time in heaven does not correlate to time here in this world. This would give a philosophical framework in which to understand the issues addressed in *Benedictus Deus*, which spoke of the temporal distinction between physical death, the saints' reception of the beatific vision, and the general resurrection, when all the saved will receive resurrected bodies. While it makes sense to speak of this progression in terms of time in heaven—asserting that the saints in heaven *already* experience the beatific vision *before* they receive their resurrected bodies—we cannot make the same assertions in terms of time in this world. We cannot say if saints have *already* received their resurrected bodies as we reckon time in this world, because time is different for us and for them.

Contrary Views from Naturalism and Buddhism

Steven Pinker holds that the belief in life after death is simply wrong and could even be pernicious. He has said, "I don't believe that there is any mind that is separate from the operation of the brain."[74] Near-death experiences can be explained by oxygen deprivation to the brain. As for being pernicious, amidst a litany of evils attributed religion, Pinker commented, "Religions have given us . . . mothers who drown their sons so they can be happily reunited in heaven. As Blaise Pascal wrote, 'Men never do evil so completely and cheerfully as when they do it from religious conviction.'"[75] Of course, Pinker also believes that consciousness is one of the things that humans simply cannot understand, so perhaps that opens a possibility for consciousness continuing after death, though not in any way that we could understand.[76] Tsongkhapa also did not believe in physical resurrection as a final blessing. The continual rebirth of a mind-stream into one of the six realms is a fundamental problem that Buddhism seeks to solve. Becoming enlightened frees one from all constraints that distinguish one individual from another, including all physicality and conceptual thinking. In en-

74. Pinker, "Steven Pinker on Human."
75. Pinker, *How the Mind Works*, 555.
76. Pinker, *How the Mind Works*, 558–61.

lightenment, all differences are erased, and the buddha-nature cannot be described by words or concepts. Contrarily, Christianity teaches that our individuality is treasured by God and will be preserved in heaven when "we will see God face to face" (1 Cor 13:12, NRSV). Just as Aquinas saw that having a body is an essential part of our human nature and so will be preserved in heaven, it seems that being in time is also a natural part of our human nature and so should be preserved in heaven.

Rather than picturing heaven as a timeless contemplation of the beauty of God, perhaps a better image is picturing heaven as glory upon glory. Paul describes a life in Christ here in this world thus: "All of us, with unveiled faces, seeing the glory of the Lord as though reflected in a mirror, are being transformed into the same image from one degree of glory to another; for this comes from the Lord, the Spirit" (2 Cor 3:18, NRSV). About life in heaven Paul writes, "For now we see in a mirror, dimly, but then we will see face to face. Now I know only in part; then I will know fully, even as I have been fully known" (1 Cor 13:12, NRSV). Should we not then picture heaven as forever progressing in knowledge and love, moving from glory to glory or from one degree of glory to another? God is infinite. We are not infinite, even in heaven. To know fully for humans is to know with our whole mind and our whole heart, with every fiber of our being. But having knowledge leads us to be able to understand more, and so knowledge can always progress. Knowledge builds on itself. While this is true here in this life, perhaps it remains true in heaven in a more pure form. While here we struggle and sometimes fall back rather than forward, there, the motion will always be toward greater knowledge and love.

Conclusions

Christians believe in a physical resurrection rather than a disembodied, mental resurrection or no resurrection at all. Time is essentially linked to physical dimensions, so Christians should also believe that there is time in heaven. One biblical way to think about this is that as we see God face to face we learn more about God, thus enabling us to see even more, and on and on, as heaven becomes glory upon glory. This is a clear distinction from the Buddhist or naturalist views of an afterlife, and it is an intentional difference that Christians have maintained throughout their history.

What Have We Learned?

In this chapter we have seen how the ideas of others can help us to think through difficult issues of our own without ever having to agree with them in a larger context. Even if we disagree with others on fundamental issues we can learn from them by coming to understand their way of picturing the world and how that leads them to believe what they believe about particular issues.

For example, we have seen how the Catholic doctrine of original sin might change in light of challenging ideas from naturalists and Buddhists. Naturalist views hold that evolution by natural selection shows how the development of humanity is unguided and has no purpose, a view that Christianity could not hold. But Christian theology could benefit by pondering the naturalist insight that if our human bodies were created by evolution, we would expect ourselves to be imperfect with complex and contrary motivations, and thus perpetually in a state described by original sin. This should move Catholics away from a romantic and scripturally unwarranted vision of life in the Garden of Eden as a real place, an actual paradise where we could have lived indefinitely if only. . . . Instead, a minimalist view of life before the fall seems more warranted. This is further reinforced when we consider the evidence that Buddhists have of beginningless nescience, reminding Christians of a fundamental truth that their theologizing about the fall often forgets—that the best is yet to come.

Similarly, the Mahayana Buddhist ideal of the bodhisattva who works to end the suffering of all sentient beings challenges Christians to rethink a view that only humans can get into heaven. What would justify such a view? As Pope Francis points out, God loves even the tiniest sparrow, which is worth almost nothing to us. To Buddhists, all sentient beings—even animals—can feel pain and love, and they all have the tathagatagarbha, the buddha-nature at their core. In this light, Christians are reminded that their analog to the tathagatagarbha, grace, is spread by God far and wide, as God provides for even the sparrow. Yet Christians also push back against the idea of tathagatagarbha as a natural potential to infinity within us, holding that the power to save us must come from without as we do not by nature have that power within ourselves. According to Christians, we are made to know and to love. But on our own, we could never know or love completely, because on our own, we cannot know and thus love God directly. We only know of God through God's effects in the world. For this reason, God used the fall to raise us up in Christ to a new life in heaven where we will see God face to face. As Aquinas explains, "God permits evil that he might draw forth some greater good. Thus, the text in Romans reads, "Where wickedness abounded, grace abounds yet more"; and in the blessing of the Paschal Candle, "O happy fault that merited so great a redeemer."[77]

All of this talk about *salvation* comes under suspicion, however, when viewed through the eyes of skeptical naturalists. How could Christians proclaim a God of infinite love and power who wants to save all people when most of the people who have ever lived have no meaningful access to their savior, Jesus Christ? Given the vast dimensions of the universe and the separation of cultures even on this planet due to the difficulty of communication throughout most of history, a plausible account needs to be offered of how a supposedly divine incarnation that took place in an obscure land before the arrival of mass communication for a mere thirty-three years could have a universal significance. We have tried to do that without having to posit what we see as an unwarranted though theologically possible multiplication of divine dispensations, taking as seriously the plight of isolated cultures on this planet as we take a theoretically isolated Martian culture.

Lastly, in contrast to both naturalism and Buddhism, we argued for an experience of time in heaven to make meaningful the belief in bodily resurrection. Sometimes insights come by adopting ideas of others, but sometimes they come from opposing them more explicitly. This final insight is a case of the latter.

If even only one of the ideas we have proposed here is adopted by the wider Christian community, the dialogue with non-Christians will have served to improve Christian theology. This dialogue has already sharpened our own theological understanding and forced us to dig deeper into issues that we thought already had simple, settled answer until new questions were raised in dialogue with others. Such is the hope of interreligious dialogue in this mode: not to convert others to our way of seeing the world, but to better our own understanding.

---

77. Aquinas, *Summa Theologiae*, 3:1.3 resp. 3. "Romans" is Paul's Letter to the Romans in the New Testament. The Paschal Candle is a symbol of Christ's resurrection that is blessed at the Easter Vigil liturgy, the high point of the church's year.

Epilogue

The three pictures of the world of Thomas Aquinas, Tsongkhapa, and Steven Pinker are quite detailed and quite different from one another in their depictions of reality. We could ask whose was the correct picture, but the answer would probably vary, with most people believing that the picture most in line with their own was the most compelling. That is part and parcel of what it means to have world-pictures. Few would agree with everything any one of these authors wrote, and that is also part of what it means to have a world-picture. As important as they are to our evaluation of the world, even conditioning the questions we care to ask about it, world-pictures are difficult to get at and, when conveyed to others, do not work well in converting them to one's own view. They are shared communally, not by discussing them directly but by living out of them with others. But world-pictures are essential to deal with if we are ever to understand other people whose world-pictures differ significantly from our own.

Fostering understanding does not usually lead to conversion, abandoning one's beliefs, and adopting the other's. Rather, it enables learning from one another and more effective collaboration in building a better world. Chapter 5 shows how much we, the authors of this book, have been enriched our own understanding of Christianity by studying Buddhist and naturalist thought. We have not ceased to be Christians; we have deepened our communal understanding of Christianity. This same dynamic has happened many times in the history of Christianity as Christians encountered new cultures and new philosophies, perhaps most famously when Aquinas entered into dialogue with the philosophy of Aristotle.

Unfortunately, examples of dialogue-gone-astray also abound in our world, even with the quality authors we have studied here. Often writers immersed in one tradition will comment on the superiority of their own tradition compared to others with very little insight into the real understanding of the other tradition. What is the point of such comparisons? To circle the wagons? To convince believers that they have backed the right horse and they do not need to investigate other views for themselves, because someone intelligent has already done this and can give you the short version of why the other is not as good? For example, in his 1994 book *Crossing the Threshold of Hope*, Pope John Paul II explains his vision of Christianity, "the meaning of salvation; about hope; about the relationship of Christianity to other faiths."[1] The other faiths do not fare so well. In a chapter on Buddhism, John Paul II notes that he has met the Dalai Lama "a few times." He then gives his summary evaluation of Buddhism as a religion:

> The "enlightenment" experienced by Buddha comes down to the conviction that the world is bad, that it is the source of evil and suffering for man. To liberate oneself from this evil, one must free oneself from this world, necessitating a break with the ties that join us to external reality—ties existing in human nature, in our psyche, in our bodies. The more we are liberated from these ties, the more we become indifferent to what is in the world, and the more we are freed from suffering, from the evil that has its source in the world.[2]

This is not a plausible description of the Buddhism of Tsongkhapa and the Dalai Lama, who believe that the goal of Buddhism is to unite wisdom and compassion in order to become enlightened and thus be able to lead others out of suffering. The view of non-abiding nirvana, where nirvana is not an escape from samsara but a re-engagement with the same reality without the grasping desires that turn it to suffering, shows a goal not of becoming free from the world but of engaging more deeply with it in a way that is helpful rather than causing more suffering.

Instead of making general claims about Buddhism, one wonders what kind of conversation they could have had if the pope had shared his views about Buddhism with the Dalai Lama and asked whether he had gotten it right. That could have been a very enlightening conversation on both sides. Having met the Dalai Lama, did John Paul II experience him

---

1. From the description of the book on the dust jacket.
2. John Paul II, *Crossing the Threshold*, 85–86.

as indifferent to the world, unengaged and lacking in compassion? That hardly seems possible.

Other examples of dialogue-gone-astray are naturalist rants against theistic religion, such as this one from Steven Pinker:

> For anyone with a persistent intellectual curiosity, religious explanations are not worth knowing because they pile equally baffling enigmas on top of the original ones. What gave God a mind, free will, knowledge, certainty about right and wrong? How does he infuse them into a universe that seems to run just fine according to physical laws? How does he get ghostly souls to interact with hard matter? And most perplexing of all, if the world unfolds according to a wise and merciful plan, why does it contain so much suffering? As the Yiddish expression says, If God lived on earth, people would break his windows.[3]

Granted, Aquinas's philosophy can be intricate and difficult, but he clearly has answers to these questions, answers that are at least worth knowing because they are worked out in fine detail. Nothing gave God anything—God is knowledge, goodness, and truth itself. How did God infuse these into the world? In something like the way a painter infuses a message into a great work of art. Could there be no message infused into the Mona Lisa because it is ultimately just daubs of paint? Aquinas criticized the idea of ghostly souls for the same reason Pinker cites, and thus he did not believe that we had them. It takes a lifetime to explore why there is suffering in the world created by a good God, and it would be well worth the effort to engage the question rather than dismiss it from the start.

Rather than standing back lobbing what he thinks are bombs that will surely destroy any theistic perspective, Pinker would do better to have a real conversation with a competent theologian. Not that he would be convinced by their answers, but he might learn something and then be able to ask better questions. There are some real problems with Aquinas and Catholic theology, but these are not them. A deeper dialogue could benefit both sides.

Perhaps finding competent dialogue partners is difficult. In his book *A Universe from Nothing*, Lawrence Krauss writes, "Indeed, I have challenged several theologians to provide evidence contradicting the premise that theology has made no contribution to knowledge in the past five hundred years at least, since the dawn of science. So far no one has provided a

---

3. Pinker, *How the Mind Works*, 560.

counterexample."[4] Two obvious counterexamples are Mahatma Gandhi and Dr. Martin Luther King. Doesn't figuring out why we should end slavery, or care about the poor, or stand against tyranny count as advancing human understanding? Passages like these do not indicate that there is a rich dialogue of ideas happening between naturalist philosophers and theologians. Perhaps this book could help to improve the situation.

Even when dialogue is pursued in depth, it can become derailed by not attending to the difference differences make. Such is the case with Matthew Dickerson's *The Mind and the Machine: What It Means to Be Human and Why It Matters*, an extended comparison of naturalist and Judeo-Christian views of the human person. Dickerson ultimately argues for the superiority of classical Judeo-Christian views that largely agree with Thomas Aquinas over naturalist views such as those espoused by Richard Dawkins and Daniel Dennett, but he has studied many views and does a good job analyzing and relating them to each other. He believes, however, that he has a knockout blow against the naturalists' assertion of their position as *true*, writing, "evolution itself is the very thing that is in conflict with naturalism—not that they can't both be true, but that one can't sensibly or reasonably believe in them both. To accept both is to deny the validity of reason itself."[5] His argument is that if you believe that the mind is limited to the physical brain, and that our brains developed through a process of natural selection to respond to the world in ways that were reproductively advantageous, then our ability to reason is simply a programmed response to the world.[6] The mind does not know what is *true*, it knows how to react successfully to the world—and if your mind can't know truth, it can't assert a theory as true.

This misses a crucial fact, however—Dickerson and Dennett have different definitions of truth. Dickerson, in agreement with Thomists, believes that truth is when our minds grasp the way the world is in itself. Naturalists such as Dennett, Dawkins, and Pinker often speak in absolutes, as if they know exactly what the world is like, but that is not really what they believe. They know that the scientific method can only judge whether particular theories successfully predict the outcomes of events in the world, and they look to the scientific method to sort out which theories perform best. But scientists all know that theories can get overturned as new data comes in. Einstein overturned Newtonian physics, and no one knows where quantum

---

4. Krauss, *Universe from Nothing*, 144.
5. Dickerson, *Mind and the Machine*, 101.
6. Dickerson, *Mind and the Machine*, 94–103.

physics will lead us. So science tells us what works in a provisional way, and ultimately, scientific naturalists affirm this and deny that anything can be known with certainty or *a priori*. A theory is true if it is the best explanation that can successfully predict the outcome of future, similar situations. So it is reasonable to assert as *true* that our brains developed through evolution, because this is the theory that best explains the data. Any other position, naturalists argue, is simply ignoring the facts or twisting them to fit a preconceived notion.

Dickerson's inattention to these different definitions of truth gets in the way of productive dialogue. Pinker believes that since our minds were developed through the mechanism of natural selection on the savannas of Africa, they do well at dealing with lions and rocks and other people, but they never developed the ability to understand questions such as what consciousness is. It would be more instructive to have Dickerson comment on Pinker's assertion of the limits to our understanding than to have to wade through a critique that doesn't address the real issues because it missed a fundamental point. The authors of this book believe in Dickerson's perspective, but, as Aquinas said, making bad arguments for one's position opens it up to mockery,[7] and the world does not need more mockery.

The good news is that it is easy to have a productive dialogue that enriches everyone involved. People are naturally curious, and want to know what is *true*. We can sometimes get locked into arguments about who is right and who is wrong about the way the world is, but with just a bit of effort and creativity, that curiosity can be redirected to try to understand, "What do *you* think is true and why?" Great learning happens when we listen to the answer to this question by people who think quite differently than we do. Not that we would necessarily adopt their position, nor even find a middle ground between their position and ours, but coming to understand these different ways of picturing the world can open us up to reevaluating overlooked possibilities of the meaning of life, the universe, and everything.

---

7. Aquinas, *Summa Theologiae*, 1:32.1.

Works Cited

Aktuell, Buddhismus, and Michael Doepke. "Interview with the Dalai Lama about the Full Ordination of Women." *Tibetan Buddhism in the West*, January, 2011. https://info-buddhism.com/Interview_Dalai_Lama_about_the_Full_Ordination_of_Women.html.

Al-Khalili, James. *Aliens: The World's Leading Scientists on the Search for Extraterrestrial Life*. New York: Picador, 2017.

Anselm of Canterbury. *Cur Deus Homo*. 2 vols. In *Complete Philosophical and Theological Treatises of Anselm Of Canterbury*, translated by Jasper Hopkins and Herbert Richardson. Minneapolis, MN: Banning, 2000.

Atheist Alliance of America. "The Richard Dawkins Award." http://www.atheistallianceamerica.org.

Augustine of Hippo. *On Marriage and Concupiscence*. New Advent. http://www.newadvent.org/fathers/1507.htm.

Austriaco, Nicanor. "The Historicity of Adam and Eve, in 4 parts." Thomistic Evolution, http://www.thomisticevolution.org/disputed-questions/.

———. "A Theological Fittingness Argument for the Historicity of the Fall of Homo Sapiens." *Nova et Vetera*, English ed. 13 (2015) 651–67.

Aquinas, Thomas. *The Compendium of Theology*. Translated by Cyril Vollert. St. Louis, MO: Herder, 1947.

———. *Commentary on the Sentences of Peter Lombard*. Latin text: Corpus Thomisticum. http://www.corpusthomisticum.org/snp1001.html.

———. *On Being and Essence*. Fordham University Medieval Sourcebook. https://sourcebooks.fordham.edu/basis/aquinas-esse.asp.

———. *On the Eternity of the World*. Fordham University Medieval Sourcebook. https://sourcebooks.fordham.edu/basis/aquinas-eternity.asp.

———. *Summa Theologiae*. 61 vols. New York: McGraw-Hill, 1965. Excerpts from the Supplement are from *Summa Theologica*. 3 vols. New York: Benzinger Brothers, 1947.

Benedict XII, Pope. *Benedictus Deus: On the Beatific Vision of God*. Papal Encyclicals Online, 1334. http://www.papalencyclicals.net/ben12/b12bdeus.htm.

Berzin, Alexander. "The Life of Tsongkhapa." Study Buddhism. https://studybuddhism.com/en/tibetan-buddhism/spiritual-teachers/tsongkhapa/the-life-of-tsongkhapa.

WORKS CITED

Brower, Jeffrey E. *Aquinas's Ontology of the Material World: Change, Hylomorphism, and Material Objects*. Oxford: Oxford University Press, 2014.

Bynum, Caroline Walker. *The Resurrection of the Body in Western Christianity, 200–1336*. New York: Columbia University Press, 1995.

Cessario, Romanus. *Christian Satisfaction in Aquinas: Towards a Personalist Understanding*. Washington, DC: University Press of America, 1982.

Dawkins, Richard. *The God Delusion*. Boston: Mariner, 2008.

———. "Steven Pinker Receives the Richard Dawkins Award at the Atheist Alliance of America convention." YouTube, October 3, 2013. https://www.youtube.com/watch?v=uciDLmA-I5k.

Dehaene, Stanislas. *Consciousness and the Brain: Deciphering How the Brain Codes Our Thoughts*. New York: Penguin, 2014.

Dennett, Daniel C. *Breaking the Spell: Religion as a Natural Phenomenon*. New York: Viking, 2006.

———. *Consciousness Explained*. Boston: Little, Brown and Co., 1991.

Dickerson, Matthew T. *The Mind and the Machine: What It Means to Be Human and Why It Matters*. Eugene, OR: Cascade, 2016.

Dugdale, John. "Richard Dawkins Named World's Top Thinker in Poll." *The Guardian*, April 25, 2013. https://www.theguardian.com/books/booksblog/2013/apr/25/richard-dawkins-named-top-thinker/.

Eberl, Jason T. "Aquinas's Account of Human Embryogenesis and Recent Interpretations." *Journal of Medicine and Philosophy* 30 (2005) 379–94.

Eckhart, Meister. *Meister Eckhart: The Essential Sermons, Commentaries, Treatises, and Defense*. Translated by Edmund Colledge and Bernard McGinn. New York: Paulist, 1981.

Einstein, Albert. *Relativity, the Special and the General Theory: A Popular Exposition*. Translated by Robert W. Lawson. London: Methuen, 1922.

Erdman, Rachel. "Sacrifice as Satisfaction, Not Substitution: Atonement in the Summa Theologiae." *Anglican Theological Review* 96 (Summer 2014) 461–80.

Flatow, Ira, with Lawrence Krauss, Simon Blackburn, Sam Harris, and Steven Pinker. "Can Science Shape Human Values? And Should It? *National Public Radio*." National Public Radio's Science Friday, November 5, 2010. https://www.npr.org/templates/story/story.php?storyId=131099083.

Francis, Pope. *Laudato Si*. The Holy See, May 25, 2015. http://w2.vatican.va/content/francesco/en/encyclicals/documents/papa-francesco_20150524_enciclica-laudato-si.html.

Freeman, Colin. "Dalai Lama Says that Any Female Successor Would Have to Be 'Attractive.'" *The Telegraph*, September 23, 2015. https://www.telegraph.co.uk/news/worldnews/asia/tibet/11885441/Dalai-Lama-says-that-any-female-successor-would-have-to-be-attractive.html.

Gribbin, John. *Erwin Schrödinger and the Quantum Revolution*. Hoboken, NJ: Wiley, 2013.

Gyamtso, Tsultrim. *Buddha Nature: The Mahayana Uttaratantra Shastra*. Translated by Rosemarie Fuchs. Ithaca, NY: Snow Lion, 2000.

Gyatso, Tenzin, Dalai Lama XIV. *Beyond Dogma: Dialogues and Discourses*. Translated by Alison Anderson. Berkeley, CA: North Atlantic, 1996.

———. *The Meaning of Life: Buddhist Perspectives on Cause and Effect*. Translated and edited by Jeffrey Hopkins. Boston: Wisdom, 2000.

———. "When Does a Stem Cell Become a Human Being? Scientific Perspectives from His Holiness the Dalai Lama." *Mandala Magazine* (March/May 2003) 14–15.

Harvey, Peter. *An Introduction to Buddhist Ethics*. Cambridge: Cambridge University Press, 2000.

Hawking, Stephen W. *A Brief History of Time: From the Big Bang to Black Holes*. New York: Bantam, 1998.

Hopkins, Jeffrey. *Tsongkhapa's Final Exposition of Wisdom*. Ithaca, NY: Snow Lion, 2008.

Jinpa, Thupten. *Self, Reality and Reason in Tibetan Philosophy: Tsongkhapa's Quest for the Middle Way*. London: RoutledgeCurzon, 2006.

John Paul II, Pope. *Crossing the Threshold of Hope*. New York: Alfred Knopf, 1994.

———. "Letter of His Holiness John Paul II to Reverend George V. Coyne, SJ, Director of the Vatican Observatory." The Holy See, June 1, 1988. https://w2.vatican.va/content/john-paul-ii/en/letters/1988/documents/hf_jp-ii_let_19880601_padre-coyne.html.

———. "Letter to Women." The Holy See, June 29, 1995. https://w2.vatican.va/content/john-paul-ii/en/letters/1995/documents/hf_jp-ii_let_29061995_women.html.

———. "Message to the Pontifical Academy of Sciences: On Evolution." *Eternal Word Television Network*, October 22, 1996. https://www.ewtn.com/library/papaldoc/jp961022.htm.

———. *Mulieris Dignitatis*. The Holy See, August 15, 1988. http://w2.vatican.va/content/john-paul-ii/en/apost_letters/1988/documents/hf_jp-ii_apl_19880815_mulieris-dignitatem.html.

———. *Ordinatio Sacerdotalis*. The Holy See, May 22, 1994. http://w2.vatican.va/content/john-paul-ii/en/apost_letters/1994/documents/hf_jp-ii_apl_19940522_ordinatio-sacerdotalis.html.

Krauss, Lawrence. *A Universe from Nothing: Why There Is Something Rather than Nothing*. New York: Atria, 2012. Kindle ed.

La Stampa. "Francis: The Pope is "a Normal Person," not Superman." *La Stampa*, March 5, 2014. http://www.lastampa.it/2014/03/05/vaticaninsider/francis-the-pope-is-a-normal-person-not-superman-h58P6IAMAANFmnJN8QxsdO/pagina.html.

Lattin, Don. "Dalai Lama Speaks on Gay Sex / He Says It's Wrong for Buddhists but Not for Society." *San Francisco Chronicle*, June 11, 1997. https://www.sfgate.com/news/article/Dalai-Lama-Speaks-on-Gay-Sex-He-says-it-s-wrong-2836591.php.

Levada, William J. "The San Francisco Solution." *First Things* 75 (August/September 1997) 17–19.

Lopez, Donald S., ed. *Buddhism in Practice*. Princeton: Princeton University Press, 1995.

Luisi, Pier Luigi. *Mind and Life: Discussions with the Dalai Lama on the Nature of Reality*. New York: Columbia University Press, 2011.

Magee, William A. *The Nature of Things: Emptiness and Essence in the Geluk World*. Ithaca, NY: Snow Lion, 2000.

McCabe, Herbert. *God Still Matters*. London: Continuum, 2002.

Namo Buddha Monastery. "The Ancient Story of Namo Buddha." http://namobuddha.org/namobuddha.html/.

New York Times. "Richard Dawkins: By the Book." *Sunday Book Review*, 12 September 2013. https://www.nytimes.com/2013/09/15/books/review/richard-dawkins-by-the-book.html.

O'Meara, Thomas F. "Paris As a Cultural Milieu of Aquinas' Thought." *The Thomist* 38 (October 1974) 689–722.

———. *Vast Universe: Extraterrestrials and Christian Revelation*. Collegeville, MN: Liturgical, 2012.
Papineau, David. "Naturalism." *The Stanford Encyclopedia of Philosophy*. Edited by Edward N. Zalta. Winter 2016 ed. https://plato.stanford.edu/entries/naturalism/.
Paul VI, Pope. *Humanae Vitae*. The Holy See, July 25, 1968. http://w2.vatican.va/content/paul-vi/en/encyclicals/documents/hf_p-vi_enc_25071968_humanae-vitae.html.
Peters, Ted. "Exotheology: Speculations on Extraterrestrial Life." In *Science, Theology, and Ethics*, by Ted Peters, 121–37. Burlington, Vermont: Ashgate, 2003.
Petri, Thomas. *Aquinas and the Theology of the Body: The Thomistic Foundations of John Paul II's Anthropology*. Washington, DC: Catholic University of America Press, 2016.
Pinker, Steven. *The Better Angels of Our Nature: Why Violence Has Declined*. New York: Penguin, 2012. Kindle ed.
———. *The Blank Slate: The Modern Denial of Human Nature*. New York: Penguin, 2016. Kindle ed.
———. "The Cognitive Niche: Coevolution of Intelligence, Sociality, and Language." Proceeding of the National Academy of Sciences of the United States of America 107, suppl. 2 (May 11, 2010) 8993–99.
———. *How the Mind Works*. New York: Norton, 1997. Kindle ed.
———. "Steven Pinker Defines Morality." *Big Think*. http://bigthink.com/videos/steven-pinker-defines-morality.
———. "Steven Pinker on Human Consciousness." YouTube, June 19, 2011. https://www.youtube.com/watch?v=2qnb9sd4DUk.
———. *The Stuff of Thought*. New York: Penguin, 2007.
———. "Three Reasons to Affirm Free Speech." Keynote Address at the Foundation for Individual Rights in Education's 15th Anniversary Dinner, New York, Oct. 23, 2014. https://www.thefire.org/three-reasons-affirm-free-speech-keynote-address-fires-15th-anniversary-dinner/.
Pinker, Steven, Matt Ridley, Alain de Bottom, and Malcolm Gladwell. *Do Humankind's Best Days Lie Ahead? The Munk Debates*. Edited by Rudyard Griffiths. House of Anansi Press, 2016. Kindle ed.
Pius XII, Pope. *Humani Generis*. The Holy See, August 12, 1950. http://w2.vatican.va/content/pius-xii/en/encyclicals/documents/hf_p-xii_enc_12081950_humani-generis.html.
Plested, Marcus. *Orthodox Readings of Aquinas*. Oxford: Oxford University Press, 2012.
Rahner, Karl. *Science and Christian Faith*. Translated by Hugh M. Riley. Vol. 21, *Theological Investigations*. New York: Crossroad, 1988.
Rahula, Walpola. *What the Buddha Taught*. New York: Grove, 1974.
Roman Catholic Church. *Catechism of the Catholic Church*. The Holy See, 1993. http://www.vatican.va/archive/ENG0015/_INDEX.HTM.
———. *Digitatis Personae*. Congregation for the Doctrine of the Faith. The Holy See, 1998. http://www.vatican.va/roman_curia/congregations/cfaith/documents/rc_con_cfaith_doc_20081208_dignitas-personae_en.html.
———. *Dominus Iesus*. Congregation for the Doctrine of the Faith. The Holy See, 2000. http://www.vatican.va/roman_curia/congregations/cfaith/documents/rc_con_cfaith_doc_20000806_dominus-iesus_en.html.
———. *Donum Vitae*. Congregation for the Doctrine of the Faith. The Holy See, 1987. http://www.vatican.va/roman_curia/congregations/cfaith/documents/rc_con_cfaith_doc_19870222_respect-for-human-life_en.html.

———. *Gaudium et Spes*. The Holy See, 1965. http://www.vatican.va/archive/hist_councils/ii_vatican_council/documents/vat-ii_const_19651207_gaudium-et-spes_en.html.

———. *Lumen Gentium*. The Holy See, 1964. http://www.vatican.va/archive/hist_councils/ii_vatican_council/documents/vat-ii_const_19641121_lumen-gentium_en.html/.

Sagan, Carl. "Flatland and the 4th Dimension." YouTube, September 6, 2014. https://www.youtube.com/watch?v=iiWKq57uAlk.

Saldon, Tenzin. "His Holiness the Dalai Lama Speaks to Delegates from the First Tibetan Women's Empowerment Conference." *Central Tibetan Administration*, February 24, 2017. http://tibet.net/2017/02/his-holiness-the-dalai-lama-speaks-to-delegates-from-the-first-tibetan-womens-empowerment-conference/.

Samuel, Geoffrey. *Civilized Shamans: Buddhism in Tibetan Societies*. Washington, DC: Smithsonian Institution Press, 1993.

Sponberg, Alan. "Attitudes toward Women and the Feminine in Early Buddhism." In *Buddhism, Sexuality, and Gender*, edited by Jose Cabezon, 3–37. Albany: State University of New York Press, 1992.

Stearns, Cyrus. *The Buddha from Dolpo: A Study of the Life and Thought of the Tibetan Master Dolpopa Sherab Gyaltsen*. Albany: State University of New York Press, 1999.

Steinkerchner, Scott. *Beyond Agreement: Interreligious Dialogue amid Persistent Differences*. Lanham, MD: Rowman & Littlefield. 2011.

Stump, Eleonore. "Atonement According to Aquinas." In *Philosophy and the Christian Faith*, edited by Thomas Morris, 61–91. Notre Dame: University of Notre Dame Press, 1988.

Svensson, Manfred, and David VanDrunen, eds. *Aquinas among the Protestants*. Hoboken, NJ: Wiley, 2017.

Torrell, Jean-Pierre. *Saint Thomas Aquinas*. Translated by Robert Royal. 2 vols. Revised ed. Washington, DC: Catholic University of America Press, 2005.

Tsongkhapa. *The Great Treatise on the Stages of the Path to Enlightenment*. 3 vols. Ithaca, NY: Snow Lion, 2002.

Turner, Denys. *Thomas Aquinas: A Portrait*. New Haven: Yale University Press, 2013.

United States Conference of Catholic Bishops. "Always Our Children: A Pastoral Message to Parents of Homosexual Children and Suggestions for Pastoral Ministers." http://www.usccb.org/issues-and-action/human-life-and-dignity/homosexuality/always-our-children.cfm.

Vanden Bout, Melissa Rovig. "Thomas Aquinas and the Generation of the Embryo: Being Human Before the Rational Soul." PhD diss., Boston College, 2013.

Wallace, B. Alan. "Why the West Has No Science of Consciousness: A Buddhist View." Presented at the conference on "Indic Contributions to a Global Renaissance," Columbia University Institute of Buddhist Studies, July 2002. http://faculty.wcas.northwestern.edu/~paller/dialogue/Wallace.pdf.

Williams, Paul. *Mahayana Buddhism: The Doctrinal Foundations*. 2nd ed. London: Routledge, 2009.

Wilson, Jeff. "All Beings Are Equally Embraced by Amida Buddha: Jodo Shinshu Buddhism and Same-Sex Marriage in the United States." *Journal of Global Buddhism* 13 (2012) 31–59.

Wittgenstein, Ludwig. *On Certainty*. Edited by G. E. M. Anscombe and G. H. von Wright. Translated by Denis Paul and G. E. M. Anscombe. New York: Harper, 1972.

www.ingramcontent.com/pod-product-compliance
Lightning Source LLC
Chambersburg PA
CBHW030113170426
43198CB00009B/604